Bobby Bowden's Tales from the Seminoles Sideline

Bobby Bowden
with Steve Ellis

Sports Publishing L.L.C.
www.SportsPublishingLLC.com

All photos in the chapter openers are by Phil Coale/Sunset Images.

Director of production: Susan M. Moyer
Developmental editor: Elisa Bock Laird
Project manager: Alicia D. Wentworth
Copy editor: Cynthia L. McNew
Photo editor: Erin Linden-Levy
Dust jacket design: Christine Mohrbacher
Imaging: Christine Mohrbacher
          Dustin Hubbart
          Heidi Norsen
Acquisitions editor: Dean Reinke
Marketing manager: Jonathan Patterson

Standard edition ISBN: 1-58261-406-7
Leather-bound edition ISBN:1-58261-958-1

Printed in the United States of America.

Sports Publishing L.L.C.
www.SportsPublishingLLC.com

(Photo by Phil Coale/Sunset Images)

Contents

Foreword

Few can tell a Bobby Bowden story as well as longtime Florida State sports information director Rob Wilson. He was present when Bowden, attempting to explain to reporters how the Puntrooskie worked, began moving chairs around in the post-game interview after the 1988 Clemson-Florida State game. Wilson was standing next to Bowden when he took a congratulatory phone call from President Bill Clinton for winning a second national championship and responded: "How come you're not working tonight?"

But maybe his two favorite stories have to do with Bowden's relationship with the media for much of his career and his dealing with assistant coaches during games.

"We're playing at Michigan," he begins. "After the game is over, the team is on the bus and ready to go. Everybody is looking at me and wondering—'Where is Coach Bowden?' I thought he was already in the trooper car, so I get out of the bus and see that he's not there.

"I go back to the locker room, and I hear the shower running. I go in, and there he is, naked as a jaybird, taking a shower. A sportswriter is standing in the shower with him fully dressed. The water is running over the writer, and Bowden is yapping away with the writer writing as fast as he can. I'll never forget that one.

"This next one was told to me by Art Baker. He was the quarterbacks coach here [in 1984]. All week before one of the games the coaches are talking about how good this one linebacker is for the other team. ... The tight end [for Florida State] is going to be ineffective.

"During the first half of the game, Coach Bowden jumps on the headset and says, 'Art, Art. Why don't we throw to the tight end?'

"And Coach Baker answers, 'Well, Coach, let me watch the coverage a couple of times.'

"Coach Bowden gets back on the headset a little later and says, 'How about that tight end?'

"Art comes back and says, 'Coach, we've talked about it all week. And I've watched the linebacker. He drops right where he is supposed to drop. We can try it, Coach. But I'm telling you the guy is in a pretty good position.'

"Coach Bowden says that maybe they can catch the linebacker flat-footed. 'Let's throw to the tight end.'

"Art replies, 'Coach, you are the boss.'

"So they call the play, and the quarterback drops back and then the tight end cuts across. And the linebacker drops where he is supposed to. The quarterback is shielded and can't see the linebacker, and the linebacker picks off the ball and returns it 30 yards.

"There is a long silence on the headsets. A long silence.

"And then Coach Bowden jumps on the headset and says, 'Art. Art.'

"And Coach Baker says, 'Yes sir, Coach?'

"And Coach Bowden says, 'I see what you mean.'"

ॐ

With more than 25 years of experience as an assistant trainer and director of sports medicine at Florida State, Randy Oravetz can fill the lunch hour with stories about Bowden. But his favorite is not a tale from the "old days" of the Bowden era, but one that took place during the 2003 season and involves Billy Smith. The retired major in the Florida Highway Patrol has missed just five game games on the sidelines in his 41 years as head of team security for Florida State. This is a story about Bowden's wit. And for those who played and worked for

Bowden, this is as much a part of him as trick plays, two national championships, a record number of wins, and a long-standing practice of confusing players' names.

Entering the Colorado game, the fourth contest of the 2003 season, the Florida State offense was already receiving heat from fans and the media for inconsistent productivity. Bowden's son Jeff was the offensive coordinator.

"It was about the fourth game of the season, and Billy is not feeling good," Oravetz says. "About 10 minutes before the team goes out on the field, I call over to see how Billy is doing. And he says, 'Look, I'm not going to make it. I'm really sick.'

"So the team goes out, and Coach Bowden is out there standing at the Seminole head [at midfield], and everybody is warming up.

"I go up to him and say, 'Coach, we have a little situation today. Billy Smith's not going to be able to come today. He'll be OK, but he just can't do it today. Do we need to get the other state trooper over here?'

"He looks around [at the stands] and says, 'No. I think I'll be OK. But you might want to get one for Jeff.'"

અ

T.K. Wetherell's first "boss" at Florida State was Bobby Bowden, his receivers coach in the mid-1960s. Bowden's last boss at Florida State will likely be Wetherell, who became the university's president in 2003. Since being named president, Wetherell has been in a position to sometimes differ with his former coach. One of those times came during the spring of 2004 when Bowden came to the defense of friend and Colorado coach Gary Barnett, whose situation included allegations of rape regarding former football players. That candid moment between Wetherell and Bowden had a link to Wetherell's first varsity game at Florida State.

"In 1965, we opened with Texas Christian," Wetherell starts. "It was my first year on the varsity, and Bobby was my coach. We had a play called the 60 Divide. On this play, I was a flanker, and I normally run the curl route or zero route. But in this particular case, they called it 60 Divide because I was supposed to run an out. We practiced that damn play, I mean all summer long. We must have run it a million times.

"I'd run an out. The tight end would run a curl, and Larry Green, our running back, would run down the middle of the seam, and Kim Hammond would throw it to him. He'd be wide open every time. It was almost guaranteed.

"It was set up in the TCU game just beautifully. It was the fourth quarter—we're behind four points. We call the 60 Divide, and I go out there and run a damn curl like I'm supposed to on a zero route and run straight into Larry Green. The ball hits him in the head, and the cornerback grabs it for an interception.

"I come off the field, and I'm thinking, 'That idiot Green ran the wrong route.' And I'm about halfway off the field—and I'll never forget this—I look up and Bowden was standing there with his hands on his hips like he does. And he says to me, 'Are you just stupid?'

"Then it hits me. 'It was the 60 Divide, idiot.' I was supposed to run an out route, and I screwed up the game. We lost 7-3.

"So every time I do something dumb in this job, I'll get a message. 'Coach Bowden called.'

"'What did he say?'

"'60 Divide.'

"So when he said something about Colorado, I sent over a message to him—'Remember 60 Divide.'"

❧

Charlie Barnes's favorite stories about Bobby Bowden come from thousands of miles of traveling the back roads and interstates of Florida. Every April, the executive director of Seminole Boosters and Bowden climb into a van and visit dozens of towns as part of the annual spring boosters tour. Barnes's favorite tale is years old, but he was reminded of it during the spring tour of 2004.

"In the spring he mentioned in passing that the biggest fight he ever had with Ann was about the time when they first got married. She bought a piano that cost about $4,000, which was more than he made in a whole year. He laughed and said, 'We talked about that for years.'

"I just assume this was a mother who wanted her children to learn how to play a piano and bring music in their lives. There were a couple of people in the van, and they asked, 'Do your kids play?'

"And he said, 'No. They took lessons, but none of them stuck to it.'

"There was this silence and finally someone asked who played it. And he answered, 'Oh. I did.'

"That's just one of those things that people don't know about him. It goes together with something a player told me later on this tour. [Former player] LeRoy Butler said later on the tour, 'One of the reasons that we respected him was that he was the only coach that could coach every position on the team.' He does a lot of things people simply don't realize.

"And one of those things is he is very musical. He has a very good light baritone voice. He has musical training and had his own band and played instruments. And he appreciates good music, which leads me to one night, many years ago, we were going from Tampa to Winter Haven. It was a black, starless night on a long, dark road with not a lot going on. That night we started talking about how they changed all the hymns from when he was young. If there is any one reason that he and I get along, it is we have a very strong dislike for change.

"I had in the car a CD of the Statler Brothers' gospel hits, and it was the old stuff we sang in church. Now we never listen to music when we travel, but he told me to put it on and we started singing. And here we are—the Statler Brothers' and Bobby and Charlie singing every song. Of the 28 years I've trav-

Bobby Bowden's love for music goes back to his youth when he played trombone. (Photo by Phil Coale/Sunset Images)

eled with him that was the time I felt closest to him and had the best time.

"And as we drove up to the hotel, the last song played and we sang the last words and got out."

Chapter *1*

Games

Part I
The Bizarre

Trick Plays Off the Field

This is a great story.

In his own words, Bobby Bowden considers the 1983 game against Tulane one of the most bizarre of his 269 victories at Florida State entering the 2004 season. That's because the victory came months after the game was played. The NCAA made Tulane forfeit the game for using an ineligible player in the Green Wave's 34-28 victory.

Yet all that came after a tumultuous weekend that went awry from the start.

We flew into New Orleans, and I'm sitting with Bill Smith, who heads our security. And Bill says, "I wonder where the buses are?"

We pull down there, and there ain't no buses. So we have to call the bus company for them to come get us. We have to wait 30 or 40 minutes. Well, the buses ain't there because the University of Central Florida arrived before us [to play Southeastern Louisiana]. Bill Peterson [a former Florida State head coach] was their athletic director, and he got our buses.

When the new buses arrived, the drivers weren't aware of a wreck that involved a semi-trailer that stopped traffic heading into the city from the airport.

That holds us up an hour and maybe two. That means we don't get to practice in the Superdome. We get to the hotel, and we ain't got rooms or maybe not as many as we're supposed to have. And it's at the hotel that Bill Smith found out that when Central Florida arrived at the airport, [our] bus driver [had] asked, "Are you the guys from Florida?"

And Bill Peterson, that rascal, said, "Yeah, we're the guys from Florida."

And they boarded our buses. So we had that and the room confusion. But it's not over. When we have our pregame meal the night before, it was out there in the open where anybody in the hotel could just walk through. You were distracted as heck. No privacy.

Then we get up and get ready for the game and find out [quarterback] Kelly Lowrey still has the flu. And there was also all that stuff going on about their quarterback [Jon English], who was the coach's son and had an eligibility question. The NCAA says, "You can't play him." And their coach, Wally English, says, "I'm going to do it anyway." And he got a court injunction.

We ain't even played the game yet.

Florida State entered the game undefeated after it edged East Carolina in a season-opening 47-46 thriller and then won 40-35 at Louisiana State in a game between top 15 teams. The Seminoles were ranked ninth when they returned to the state of Louisiana to face unranked and heavy underdog Tulane. Florida State trailed 31-28 until Tulane sealed the game on a 40-yard field goal with a minute remaining.

But Bowden knew his team was in trouble on the opening drive when Tulane's Treg Songy returned an interception 99 yards for a touchdown.

Now the turning point in the game was when we got down on their three-yard line, and we threw a pass toward the end zone and they intercepted. He ran it nearly 100 yards for a touchdown. Kelly had to chase that guy for 80 yards, and he was dead.

In addition to an energy-draining flu bug, the Florida State quarterback had a bit of a gut.

He had gotten big. He had gotten to 218, and we thought it was too heavy—"Kelly, you are 218 and you got to get under that."

I'd ask Kelly how much he weighed, and he'd always say, "218." We'd ask him again, and he would reply, "218." So we finally get him on the scales, and he weighs 238.

Anyway, they intercepted that pass, and they beat us.

But that's not the end to the Tulane story.

I had this ring that Ron Clark of Palatka had given me [on a stop during the annual spring boosters tour]. Woo, it was a pretty thing. A garnet and gold ring—the garnets spelled FSU. I took a shower and laid it down. I was one of the last to get out. When I came back to my locker, it was gone.

And still, there is more. Two years later, with Florida State set to open the 1985 season at Tulane—its first trip back since the 1983 debacle, Bowden returned to Palatka, where the club gave him an expensive handcrafted knife by world-acclaimed craftsman Steve Swartzer.

Bowden remembers being surprised by the knife. But without any hesitation, he knew exactly what to say when Swartzer presented it to him.

I told them, "I'm going to take this knife, and I'm going back to New Orleans and find that dadgum ring."

The Palatka group roared with laughter.

Thumbs Up

Here's another bus story. There was that time our bus was coming back from Thomasville, [Georgia,] and it broke down. That was 1978. We stayed in Thomasville on Friday nights like we do now. The next day, we had our pregame meal about four o'clock up there, and we get on our buses to come to the stadium to play Cincinnati. Our bus broke down, and we couldn't get it started. We were about two-thirds of the way here. Every player on that bus thumbed, and I think I thumbed, too.

Before home games, there was a lot of traffic, so everybody found rides, but they all came in at different times. Finally, all our players got back to the stadium.

We got behind Cincinnati 21-20 in the fourth quarter. We weren't into it at all. I think all of that trying to get back to the stadium affected us. It took us out of our routine. We had that big fourth down and about 20 yards, and Jimmy Jordan is at quarterback and finds Sam Platt for a [54-yard] touchdown with a minute and a half to play.

Florida State, despite its transportation setback, won 26-21.

A Busted Gas Tank and a Blown Gasket

Bowden recalls another game during the 1983 season that was nearly as strange. Pittsburgh was unranked when it hosted Florida State on October 8. But the Panthers featured plenty of talent, including future NFL standout Bill Fralic, who anchored Pittsburgh's offensive line. Fralic came up big. Florida State's Philip Hall kicked a field goal to cut down the Pittsburgh lead to 17-16. The Panthers took over with 8:29 on the clock and ran off 19 plays, including six for first downs. Florida State never got the ball back.

We could not get the ball away from them. They ate up eight and half minutes. Gol-ly.

Defensive assistant coach Jim Gladden remembers Bowden being more than just a little upset.

"Coach gets furious—'If you're not going to stop them, let 'em score so I can get the ball back. I don't want to die a slow death,'" Gladden says Bowden said.

The loss was devastating for Bowden, whose dislike for losing to Pitt had roots in his days as an assistant and head coach at West Virginia. It wasn't his first such reaction to defeat, but this time his wife, Ann, had not made the trip to Pittsburgh. The late Bill McGrotha, the *Tallahassee Democrat*'s longtime sports columnist, took her spot, and he quickly nodded off to sleep.

She consoles me. When you get beat like that, you are looking for somebody, and in my case, it's always Ann. Ann's a good sounding board. Ann can give me a pretty good feeling with what is happening, with what people are saying. She is a pretty good springboard for what I should do. She might question me about why I do this or that, but she usually defends me.

Without Ann's reality check, Bowden was still in a funk when he stepped off the charter jet at Tallahassee's old airport and went to his automobile. Bowden put the car into drive and proceeded to drive straight over the concrete parking dividers.

I thought there was nothing in front of me, but I was supposed to back out. I took off and ripped the bottom of that dang gas tank and spewed gas. I remember John Eason said he was afraid something was going to happen bad to me.

Eason, Florida State's wide receivers coach at the time, was one car behind as Bowden approached the airport's ticket booth. Eason firmly told Bowden to park his car and gave him a ride home.

I don't know why I was so mad.

Ann Bowden has provided love and support for Bowden throughout his coaching years. Here they share a victory kiss after Florida State won the 1993 national title. (Photo by Phil Coale/Sunset Images)

Watching Pitt play a serious game of keep-away at the end certainly had something to do with it. And Bowden just hates to lose.

"Losses hurt more than a win makes you feel good," he told the *Tallahassee Democrat* years later during a rare five-loss season in 2002.

He admits that the football demons still keep him up at night after a game. But he can't recall ever being in such a funk as he was after that 1983 loss to Pittsburgh.

Not any more. Not like that one.

They Got Every Break in the Book

Of course, the '93 title game had that bizarre ending. That was the oddest thing in the world. Oh, how odd that was. I was there on the sidelines, and we had just kicked a field goal to go ahead 18-16 with 21 seconds remaining in the game.

They get the ball. Tommie Frazier throws a pass, and we tackle the receiver and put him on the ground and the clock was out. So we won it.

In a game between the nation's top two ranked teams, in the 1994 Orange Bowl with a first-ever national title on the line for Bowden and Nebraska's Tom Osborne, Scott Bentley had seemingly sealed it for Florida State with his 22-yard field goal.

But a penalty for unsportsmanlike conduct and a return to Nebraska's 43-yard line gave the Cornhuskers the ball in good field position but with little time to strike. Frazier's first attempt to Trumane Bell was incomplete. But his next pass to Bell was good for 29 yards and put the ball at the 28-yard line. It didn't seem to matter; time expired. Florida State rushed out to the field in celebration. Bowden looked for Osborne.

We start to come off the field that first time, and they hit me in the head with that stinkin' ice [from the POWERade bath]. I don't know if people realize it or not, but that liked to knock me out. He racked me good, boy. They hit me with that bucket in the head. If you look at the film, I start to go down. Gosh, that hurt.

We go out there to around midfield, and I start to shake hands with Tom; the crowd is all around us. And the official comes up there and says, "Coach Bowden, we got to put one more second on the clock."

I said, "Where is the ball?" And they said on something like the 33-yard line. Well, their kicker had never kicked one over 47 yards. I knew what his range was, and this was going to be five yards further than that—50 or maybe more. So I'm thinking, "No sweat. This kid can't kick one over 47 yards."

Bowden is bathed in POWERade in a premature victory celebration at the 1994 Orange Bowl that eventually gave Florida State its first national championship. The celebration was more pain than fun for Bowden. The bucket nailed him on the back of the head. (Photo by Phil Coale/Sunset Images)

Now we're back on the sidelines and the official comes up to me again and says, "Coach, we were wrong. We got to move the ball up five more yards. The press box said the ball was supposed to be up here."

And now I'm thinking, "Now they are in range." Can you believe this? Not only did they get one second back, but they got five yards out of it. It was really unbelievable. The things you don't want to happen were happening. You're trying to get everybody focusing on the kick, trying to block that kick. I didn't really say anything to the officials. They call what they see, and once they call it, that's the way it is.

I just remember people behind me were cussing the officials. Administrators. There were some upset people on the sidelines. It

Bowden, left, is told by the referee that there is one second left in the game and that Nebraska will get one more play, a field goal opportunity that could win the game. Florida State athletic director Bob Goin, right, listens to the conversation. (Photo by Phil Coale/Sunset Images)

did cross my mind, "Good gracious, we could lose this thing on all of this."

We've had some bad luck in some of these national championship games. The fact Chris Weinke couldn't play against Tennessee in the Fiesta Bowl [in 1999]. And against Oklahoma [in the 2001 Orange Bowl], we didn't have "Snoop" [Marvin Minnis]. But against Nebraska, we had a little of both [kinds of luck], but more of the good kind.

Bowden was not the only one in disbelief. Brad Scott, Florida State's offensive coordinator who had just accepted the head coaching job at South Carolina, was nearly in shock.

"If you had time to think about it, it would have probably made you sick to your stomach," Brad Scott says. "Coach Bowden had been so close. And now he's won it, and it's going to be taken away from him."

Nebraska's Byron Bennett prepared for his 45-yard field goal attempt.

The kick went wide left. And Florida State won a national championship because of a missed field goal in the Orange Bowl, where it had known so much heartache over the years at the hands of the University of Miami. After the game, Bowden said, "We won twice."

There wasn't much to that second time we went out to the field. I don't know if I'll ever jump and holler. Now maybe that second [national championship in the 2000 Sugar Bowl]—that was pretty meaningful to me. That first one, all it did was get the monkey off my back.

That second one, we were first in the nation every day that year. It's the biggest prize out there for a coach—to win a national championship. You have to have one to fulfill your career. And not everybody gets one. Bo Schembechler never got one, and he's one of the best coaches out there.

But you ask the question, what's more important to my resume—to have a national championship or be the winningest coach, it's probably to be the winningest coach because it stands alone. But if I won more national championships than anybody else, I believe I'd prefer that.

A Cold One

Of course, when he arrived at Florida State in 1976, most football observers figured Bowden had no more than a snowball's chance in hell to turn around a Florida State program that had just four total victories in the three previous seasons.

But thanks to real snowballs at North Texas State in his first season, hell for Florida State opponents soon followed. That November 1976 game in a snowstorm could easily rank with the 1983 games at Tulane and Pittsburgh as Bowden's most bizarre games at Florida State. Instead, he calls it his most fun and one of the most important for the Seminoles.

That's probably my all-time favorite game in 28 years. That was the game that turned us around. The reason I say that is we were 2-6 going into our last three games—Southern Mississippi, North Texas State, and Virginia Tech. We were probably going to lose all three of them. That first year, we weren't very good.

That finish, I believe, gave our boys confidence and our fans hope. In my opinion, it started us out on our success story.

Bowden and his team woke up that morning in Denton, Texas, staring at five inches of snow. Wintry weather, in part, had chased West Virginia University coach Bowden from Morgantown, West Virginia, to Tallahassee in 1976. Bowden polled his players that morning in Denton. About 80 percent were seeing their first snow. Bowden's pregame speech had little to do with strategy.

I told them, "There's nothing we can do about this but have fun."

The weather was in favor of North Texas State and its coach, Hayden Fry, who later led Iowa to great success. Bill Snyder, who went on to coach Kansas State, was an assistant coach under Fry.

Cold weather and Florida State don't usually mix. A young Bowden, and his sister, Marion, didn't like cold weather or snow when they were growing up any more than the Florida State players did in 1976. But the Seminoles still managed to pull off a win at snowy North Texas State. (Photo courtesy of Bobby Bowden)

We were freezing while warming up the day before the game. Just cooold. But it was a pretty day. We wake up the next morning, five inches of snow. Mr. Frank [DeBord, the Florida State equipment manager,] went into town and bought every pair of gloves he could find. He bought hoods, scarves, everything he found for us to be warm.

It's their homecoming, but they had probably just 50 people there. It's still snowing, and they were thinking of calling off the game. We pull up in the bus, and we're looking down on the field, and all you could see was white except two goalposts sticking up. You couldn't see lines or nothin'. They took highway safety cones and stuck one in the corner of the end zones and one on 10-yard lines all the way down the field so you had cones outlining the end zones and the sidelines.

One of the funniest things that happened that I'll never forget is we had a fourth-and-one and they stopped us. The official said, "They stopped you," and I replied, "I want a measurement."

I made them push the snow away and find the line.

Florida State trailed 20-13 before a seven-yard touchdown run by Jeff Leggett set up a game-winning two-point conversion with just over two minutes remaining. Running back Larry Key hit Kurt Unglaub on a pass called by offensive coordinator George Haffner, and Florida State won 21-20. Along the way, the team's slowest receiver, Unglaub, went slip-slidin' away from North Texas State defenders for a 91-yard touchdown in the third quarter.

To this day, when I see Kurt, I laugh with him about it. In the last three games of that season, we have four touchdowns over 90 yards. Four—that's really something. Now Kurt goes down in history as one of the slowest receivers we ever had, but he had good hands. Well, he catches two of them. That's the oddest thing. The one he caught in the snow, he ran all the way out of the end zone because he wanted to make sure he had it. I have just great memories over that game.

Gladden said afterward, the players and the entire coaching staff, Bowden included, rolled down the bank. Players made snow angels and despite being a team full of Floridians, not one did it face-down.

Bobby Bowden credits legendary Georgia Tech coach Bobby Dodd for two lessons—one of which he put to practice against North Texas State. The lesson was that Dodd always encouraged his players to have fun.

And the second lesson lives on in Bowden's first name: Bobby. If not for the success Dodd enjoyed while Bowden was a young coach at South Georgia College, he would be known today as Robert. Bowden, at his wife's urging, considered going back to his first name of Robert early in his career because "Bobby" wasn't a name that seemed to command respect. But because Dodd had won a national title in 1952, Bowden figured "Bobby" would do just fine.

As for the way Dodd dealt with his players, he was a coach who would let his players have fun in practice. He was the first I heard of letting his boys practice with no pads on. Sometimes he would have his team go out and play volleyball. They were still vicious, but he brought a relaxed atmosphere.

There are times when you just got to do that.

A snowy day at North Texas State was one.

We had a good time.

Part II

Good Times and Even Better Memories

Trading Places

Bowden admits he wasn't sure how long the good times would last at Florida State.

Trepidations about Florida State's future weighed heavily on Bowden as he took his undefeated Seminoles to Baton Rouge, Louisiana, to face Louisiana State in late October 1979. Bowden had an offer to become LSU's new coach at the end of the season after Charlie McClendon stepped down. LSU had retreated from its heyday in the late 1950s under Coach Paul Dietzel, but the program still had great appeal for Bowden, who was raised on Southern football.

And Bowden, well into his fourth season at Florida State, still wasn't sure what to make of the Seminoles' football future despite an upbeat end to his inaugural 1976 season and two winning seasons after that.

At that time Florida State wasn't thought of. I had the support here, but it was kind of like Southern Mississippi—do you think they can do it? No. Cincinnati? No. Well, I was kind of in a quandary in Tallahassee, because I'm not sure we can do it. It wasn't just my thinking but anybody's thinking. It was like, "Bobby, if you get the LSU job, take it."

Dietzel, then the athletic director of LSU, had inquired in early September about Bowden's interest in the job.

Bowden is honored by Governor Rubin Askew (far left) after leading Florida State to its first undefeated regular season under his leadership. (Photo courtesy of Bobby Bowden)

He said, "You know this is Charlie's last year, and I would like to interview you for the job. I think you got a real good chance of getting it. I've already talked to the governor; I've talked to the [university] president."

And I said, "I might be interested, but I really wouldn't be interested in doing anything until after the season." He would call me back every two weeks. He said, "Now when I call you, if they ask who this is, I'm going to say this is your brother, Paul."

So I would get some calls from brother Paul now or then. So finally, the week before we went to play them, he called me and said, "Look, we want you."

Bowden told Dietzel he would think about it.

We liked Tallahassee and didn't want to leave. But I wasn't really sure if I could do anything here.

Florida State, undefeated after seven games, entered the game against LSU, which was just 4-2.

I told Ann, "If we go in with this undefeated football team and we can't beat them, they might just be a better program. We'll never be able to beat them. If they beat us, I just might take the job. But if we beat them, hey, maybe we can be as good as them."

We go over there and beat them 24-19. So we come back to Tallahassee, and I talked to athletic director John Bridgers and the president and tell them that I'm going to stay. I signed a new contract [$46,000 annual base salary with a 10 percent salary increase the next year] soon after November 5.

It would not be the only time that a school or an NFL team inquired about Bowden's availability.

I was contacted by a couple of NFL clubs. I've never revealed who they were. I secretly went up to Georgia, and you can imagine who that was—the Falcons. I met with the owner of the Falcons up on a farm and talked one morning in about '86.

Back in those days, every time a college job would come open, I would get a call. Southern Cal, Notre Dame. They would call and say, "Can we consider you a candidate?" And I had made up my mind at this time that this is where I wanted to stay. The one exception was Alabama. In '86, I thought my calling was to go back to Alabama. They contacted me about an interview, and I told them I didn't want to interview. I said, "If you're offering me the job, I'll talk to you. I have a job. I don't want to try out for a job." So I thought they were offering me the job and wanted me to meet some of the higher-ups the morning after we played in that All-American Bowl in Birmingham. But there were about 15 other people there, and they asked me a million questions. I was upset that I had gone through that interview.

But I have to give the Alabama president credit for tipping me off that I was not the leading candidate. When I got back home and found out I was just a candidate, I took my name out of it.

Four years later, they offered me the job after Bill Curry had left. Hootie Ingram, who was our athletic director here and then [went to] Alabama, called me. I was in Hawaii, and a big Alabama booster paged me in the Honolulu airport, and I was told, "We'll pay you whatever you got to have." Then Hootie called me, and I said, "No, I'm going to stay at Florida State."

Of course, I'm glad I did.

Entering his 29th year as head coach of Florida State, Bowden is more convinced than ever that this has been the perfect fit. He would get no argument from the most recognized of Florida State's players.

"He's a good man. He's a legend," Deion Sanders says while attending Florida State's 2004 spring game. "When you think of Florida State, you think of Coach Bowden. That's it. Nothing else."

I think a lot of it is my background. My background is deeply Southern, and Tallahassee is very much that way—more than Miami or Tampa. There is a fit there. It fits my pattern. When I was a kid, I wasn't big and I played with bigger guys. I went to a small college and had to play big schools. I went to South Georgia College, my first head-coaching job. It is a junior college, and we played four-year colleges. I was the head coach of West Virginia, and we were in the shadow of Pitt, Penn State, and Ohio State, and we were the underdog again. And at Florida State it was the same way.

Cornhusking

Only one time can I remember doing this—where I walked around a stadium before a game to get a sense of what we were fix-

Bowden always admired the football tradition Nebraska had. He and Tom Osborne talk after a 1988 meeting. (Photo by Phil Coale/Sunset Images)

ing to be a part of. My intention was to see how the people were acting. I had always heard about the sellouts for 30 years in a row and people waiting for Nebraska tickets until somebody died. Nobody knew who I was back in those days, so I just walked around unnoticed. We always arrive two hours before kickoff. I had never been there, so I got dressed and I walked all the way around the stadium just to see the Nebraska crowd. I was infatuated with Nebraska.

Bowden wasn't new to facing national powerhouses or stepping onto hallowed football grounds when the Florida State team bus arrived at Memorial Stadium in Lincoln, Nebraska, in 1980. But this was Nebraska, and the team was ranked No. 3 at that. It was the highest-ranked opponent that a Bowden-coached team at Florida State had played up to that point. And until that day, Florida State had never defeated such a high-ranking opponent.

Beating Nebraska, I thought it was a feather in your cap. I still get fired up when we play somebody like that in a traditional stadium.

After I walked around, Tom Osborne came by our locker room just to greet us and see that everything was OK and to see that we got everything we needed. That had never happened before. And not since at any other place.

Nebraska had its No. 3 ranking and tradition. Florida State was ranked No. 16 and had walk-on center Jerry Coleman, who was not only making his first start, but was also seeing his first varsity action. And he played with a hip pointer suffered early in the game.

Terry Bowden was a volunteer coach at Florida State that season and later became the head coach at Auburn. He says the staff was in a quandary as to what to do at center after its experiment with another offensive lineman, Redus Coggin, failed at Miami the previous week.

"Coleman was a walk-on, scout-team center—a terrible athlete," Terry Bowden says. "They had to decide whether to take an athlete from down the line and make him snap the ball and block some, or take [Coleman] and just have him snap. Coaches could not believe they were going to start Jerry Coleman—it was incredible.

"Jerry Coleman never blocked a soul against Nebraska, but he never had a fumbled snap and we won. Dad gave him a full scholarship, but he never played much again."

By game's end, Florida State had an 18-14 victory that wasn't sealed until the final seconds when linebacker Paul Piurowski forced a fumble that was recovered by Florida State teammate Garry Futch.

For us to go in there the first time and beat 'em, what a thrill it was. We'd just lost to Miami 10-9. You had Tom Osborne and a team used to winning. The atmosphere. And to go up there and win that dang thing without a center.

That game showed you the importance of kicking and defense. They had us 14-3 at the half. Our quarterback would drop back and pass, and their nose guard would run right over our center and make a tackle. In the second half we started sprinting out—hoping he would go the wrong way. I bet you at the half we had minus 58 yards in sacks. We couldn't block.

The second half our defense is playing ball, boy. Sam Platt scored on a six-yard run, and Bill Capece kicked four field goals. And [Rohn] Stark averaged nearly 50 yards of punting. That was a really satisfying win. That put us on the map from a national standpoint, because back in those days teams didn't beat Nebraska at Nebraska. Nobody could—maybe Oklahoma some.

A week later, Florida State defeated another third-ranked team. Pittsburgh featured Dan Marino and Hugh Green, but Florida State won 36-22 in Tallahassee.

Together with beating Pitt the next week, these are two of the most surprising wins. We were the only team to beat Pitt that year.

They also count as our best back-to-back victories—at least during my time here.

A Victory over Florida Designed on a Napkin

The game that is most satisfying to me personally—it is definitely that one against Nebraska in 1980.

That had more of a national impact. But as far as a state impact and prestige in your own state, beating Florida down there [in Gainesville] for our first time in 1977 and the first time for the program in 10 years, that was very, very big.

The thinking down there was—"Who is Florida State? Well, they're nobody." Florida had the most talent of anybody in the country. The more I look back at that game I see the importance of it for our program and the prestige of the program.

When I left Florida State in 1966 [as an assistant], we had played them three years and beat them in '64. The one thing I learned was this was the big rival. So when I came back to Florida State, one of the first things I said in my interview is that we will never be accepted here until we beat those guys down the road. The first time [in 1976] we play them, we lose by seven. The next year we go down there and win, and that was kind of exciting. But then we won four in a row, and I don't get the sense that it's that big a deal. We beat them four times—so what? Then we lost about five in a row, and then you realize how big it was—how significant that first win [in '77] was.

In that game, Bowden turned a rather standard play into another one of his tricks. Florida State was ahead 17-9 early in the third quarter with the football on its 12-yard line and facing a third-and-30 situation.

Sometimes an unexpected call is the same as a trick play with all those gadgets.

Florida State called a draw, and Larry Key broke loose for 38 yards and a first down. Florida State went on to win 37-9. More than 5,000 fans greeted Florida State that evening in Doak Campbell Stadium after the Seminoles earned their ninth victory of the season—which tied the school record for wins in a regular season.

One of the biggest victories in Florida State history had an inauspicious start on an Ocala/Silver Springs Holiday Inn napkin. Bowden's staff members were sipping their morning coffees, waiting for the pregame meal to begin. Bowden, oblivious to his surroundings, was writing notes or doodling—defensive assistant coach Jim Gladden wasn't sure which until Bowden was done. On the napkin, Bowden had scribbled the offensive plays that he wanted to open with against Doug Dickey's Gators. It was a far cry from the process later developed of scripting plays and holding Friday night "iffy sessions" in which every possible situation is discussed the night before a game.

Gladden recalls there being at least eight plays on the napkin. Bowden remembers two. Both agree on the results. "We ripped them with those plays—I mean ripped them," says Gladden.

They worked pretty good.

To this day, the first two plays have stuck with Bowden.

I can remember sitting there with that napkin, thinking, "If we do this on the first play and do this on the second play, it just might be a touchdown." We run two plays and score on the second. I can remember 'em. We started off with what we call 3-44-Z-Curl. We hit Mike Shumann for first down. The second play, we fake that play and Wally [Woodham] hits ol' Unglaub on a corner route [for a 37-yard touchdown]. He got wide open—catching that thing over his shoulders and going right into the end zone. So we score on two plays.

It's not something I'd do a lot of now, but I may do that occasionally. Something might hit me before the game, where I'll go up to [son] Jeffrey and say, "I want you to run this on the first play." And I've had them hit before.

One Too Many

Now one of the greatest accomplishments is when we beat the Gators out here in 1996. That would have been one of the best-

coached games since I've been here—or best-played games, because coaches are not any better than how their kids play.

They had two receivers who went first round in the NFL draft [in 1997]. They had [Danny] Wuerffel. The big thing people don't realize, still can't seem to put together, is that you win with defense. They were the No. 1 football team in the country, and Mickey [Andrews, Florida State's defensive coordinator] just shut them down. We were able to score enough points to beat them. But our defense was terrific. I called the offense for years—it's kind of what I'm known for or associated with—but I've always believed in defense. Since I began coaching, the defense comes first, and that's why it's so important having somebody like Mickey. Our biggest wins have been defensively. Occasionally, the offense pulls it out.

Bowden rates that edition of the Gators among the most talented teams he has faced while at Florida State. The contest is one of six times that Florida State has been involved in a game between the Associated Press's top two teams—all under Bowden. At the time, it was just the fourth meeting in NCAA Division I-A history between two undefeated teams in the regular-season finale, a bout the Seminoles won 24-21.

In a rematch with the national championship at stake, Florida easily handled Florida State 52-20 in the Sugar Bowl later that season. But on November 30, Bowden's Seminoles beat the Gators in Doak Campbell Stadium.

Warrick Dunn rushed for 185 yards and set up Florida State's winning touchdown midway through the fourth quarter. Wuerffel, the eventual Heisman Trophy winner that season, passed for 362 yards and three touchdowns while under heavy pressure from Florida State's defense. Florida coach Steve Spurrier quickly cried foul—claiming that the Seminoles had battered Wuerffel with late hits.

It was a controversy that would stay alive when the two teams met in a rematch in the Sugar Bowl.

The one thing I remember about it, and kind of halfway admired him for it, is when [Spurrier] complained so much about late hits. Now he shocked me on television—I didn't know it was coming.

Now when we played each other in the Sugar Bowl, before that game, we're at a bowl event together. As we walked off the stage together, he said, "You know the reason I did that was to let my boys know that I'm going to protect them."

I said, "Yeah, I know."

He was doing that to protect his boys. That's nearly like with the twisted knee [incident involving Darnell Dockett and a tackle he made in the 2001 Florida State-Florida game]. It's kind of like he is telling his players, "When we play them again, the officials are going to remember this, and they are going to protect us."

While the late-hit debate raged on publicly at the 1997 Sugar Bowl, Florida State had bigger concerns. Linebacker Daryl Bush and defensive end Peter Boulware had been hit with flu-like symptoms. Both spent the night before the game vomiting, yet both played after getting IVs during the game, and Bowden says he sought to keep that news quiet. With changing federal laws regarding students' privacy, Bowden says he still tries to be forthcoming with injuries, but there are exceptions.

I usually shoot pretty straight on that, but there are times where it's just not fair to the kid to let somebody know about a player's injury or health.

Spurrier wasn't so hush-hush when it came to the late hits. But whether Spurrier's comments had an effect on the officiating crew isn't known, and Bowden concedes it didn't matter.

It wasn't going to be easy beating a team that good twice in a row. It's just a shame we had to play them twice.

"This Is Too Good"

Bowden has four ties at Florida State, including two during the 1984 season and a 31-31 tie against Florida in Doak Campbell Stadium in 1994 that Bowden admits feels more like a win.

The Choke at Doak—the greatest Florida State comeback during the Bowden era—remains vivid in the memory of Florida State fans. Down 31-3, the Seminoles scored 28 points in the final 13 minutes. Highlights included Danny Kanell's pass to Kez McCorvey on fourth and 10. James Colzie diving to intercept a Wuerffel pass that led to Florida State tying the score. And Warrick Dunn's move on two Gators during Florida State's final scoring drive, which culminated with Rock Preston running into the end zone with under two minutes remaining.

That was an amazing thing. They had us 24-3 at halftime, and I can remember some of the things I said to our men.

"Now, we ain't done. If they can score 24 in the first half, we can score 24 in the second half. But men, we have got to stop them and then we got to score."

That kind of approach with the boys is natural to me. I've always had that confidence in us where if they score this many points, we can too. I'll take notes of what I'm observing during a game. And during the game I probably spotted something in the boys. A lot of times when we're behind like that, I'll want to stay calm and set the tone of how we're going to turn it around. [You know,] "We got to do this and this, and I know we can."

Whereas if things are going real good, you better get on them because they are going to get lax. If you're blowing somebody out or you're playing great, everybody wants to celebrate. That's where you might jump on them more.

Receiver McCorvey says the tone in which Bowden delivered his speech stirred the team.

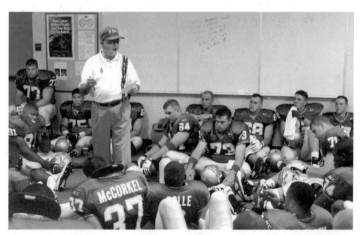

Bowden is known for his ability to connect with his team in the lock-er room. (Photo by Phil Coale/Sunset Images)

"The biggest thing was he had a calm voice," McCorvey recalls. "He didn't berate us. No panic in his voice."

Florida State, trailing by 21, kicked off to Florida in a packed Doak Campbell Stadium.

So we kick off to them, and they score. Now you figure, it's all over. You're thinking, "This is going to be embarrassing. How bad is this going to be?" But that dang thing rocks back and forth. We got Warrick Dunn on flares, and he kept getting first downs. And then the crowd gets into it. They could not stop us, and [Spurrier] won't stop throwing. And our defense makes some things happen off that. James Colzie got a couple of interceptions. And then Rock Preston scores.

And with 1:45 remaining, the coach who can't stand ties had to choose.

Then comes the decision whether to go for two. I can't afford to blow this; this is too good. We came back from 31-3. Let's ensure a tie.

The decision came without protest from his players. Even Derrick Brooks, known at Florida State and later as an All-Pro with the NFL's Tampa Bay Buccaneers for an insatiable appetite to win, embraced a late November tie.

"We did something unprecedented. We all understood that," Brooks says. "Coach Bowden felt that we battled back so hard he didn't want us to lose. It was just as sweet as a victory."

Bowden concurs.

It's a tie, but really it should be among my favorite wins, because it felt like a win. There's probably nobody better we love to beat than [Spurrier] since I've been here. I guess I enjoyed that tie as much as any win I've ever had.

But that tie did not make Bowden break into song as he did after Florida State defeated the Gators 23-12 without Chris Weinke in 1998. Weinke's serious neck injury forced Florida State coaches to turn to seldom-used Marcus "Rooster" Outzen in the final two games of the regular season. Against Florida, Outzen threw for just 213 yards but played well enough for the victory and the invitation to play Tennessee for the national title in the Fiesta Bowl.

Everybody is in the locker room, and I just had to sing the rooster song. That was a fraternity song. In World War II songs like that were sung by the troops. And when the guys went home after the war and into schools, they probably sung it in their faternities. The song went:

"We had a chicken,
"No eggs would it lay.
"One day a rooster came into our yard
"And caught that chicken right off its guard."

Florida State players got a kick out of Bowden singing the rooster song after Florida State beat Florida in 1998. But they shouldn't have been surprised by his musical talent; he (circled) played the trombone in high school. (Photo courtesy of Bobby Bowden)

And then they would all yell,
        "They are laying eggs now,
        "Just like they use ter,
        "Ever since that rooster came into our yard."

In Time, One to Remember

The 38-34 last-minute victory over Florida to end the 2003 regular season had all the ingredients of a game that Bowden should count among his most memorable. It is one that Bowden said in time will join victories over Florida in 1977; 1990, Spurrier's first at Florida; and 1996.

It featured an impressive Florida State rally, a gutsy call by his staff, a winning 52-yard touchdown pass with 55 seconds remaining, and a controversy over officiating.

But a game that gave Florida State a 10-victory season after a two-year drought is too recent for Bowden to put up there with other impressive road victories. Bowden admits it took more than a half-dozen years to appreciate the importance of his first win in 1977 over Florida.

The archrivals exchanged leads four times in the fourth quarter. Quarterback Chris Rix found Dominic Robinson for 24 yards on fourth and 14 with just over a minute to play. Rix's next pass, completed to P.K. Sam in the end zone with 55 seconds remaining, gave Florida State the victory.

It don't stand out to me that way right now. If it had been an undefeated season or a national championship, maybe. But I'll say this, wins down there [in Gainesville] are very big. You get down the road from last year's win, and you start looking back and see it's a pretty big win.

That was a mighty exciting game, and important, too. Jeffrey and them called nearly all of those big passes at the end. I did tell them late in the game to hit Robinson on crossing routes. I was on the headsets, but they called most everything.

I wasn't real confident we [would come back]. I didn't take time to weigh the odds. But just think of the times we've been down there [in Gainesville] and needed one last drive. When we played down there [before], we had the ball with time to win it and threw interceptions. But you got to stay confident—"We can do it now. We just got to do this and this."

But down inside you're thinking, "We let this one get away."

Part III
Hurricane Season

But He Played Miami

Bobby Bowden used to say that it was a shame that his teams had to play Miami—even once. Bowden's Florida State teams have lost to Miami 18 times, more than to any other opponent, and seven times by three or fewer points. And many of them were games for the ages—full of big-name players and big-time plays. But too many times, a loss to Miami cost Florida State a shot at the national championship.

Bowden even joked once that the epitaph on his tombstone would read: "But he played Miami."

So it's perhaps predictable that Bowden's most memorable Miami game was a defeat.

Well, it would be the one we lost out here in our own stadium in 1987. That was a great, great football game

You had that exciting finish [in which a two-point conversion failed for Florida State]. There were so many great players out there. We had [Marion] Butts, Sammie Smith, [Pat] Tomberlin, and Ronnie Lewis. They had the Blades, and so many future NFL players were on the field, which always seems the case with these two teams. The weather was beautiful, and there was a lot of hard hitting.

I don't know if there is a series anywhere—maybe Michigan State-Notre Dame—where there is more hard hitting. If we hadn't played Miami all those times, we would have a couple of more national championships. You look at all those teams that dropped Miami. Penn State played them and dropped them. Notre Dame drops them. Florida drops them. We got to play them every year.

With Miami players celebrating in the background, Florida State placekicker Gerry Thomas walks dejectedly off the field after missing a field goal that would have won the game in 1991. (Photo by Phil Coale/Sunset Images)

Among fans, the Florida State-Miami series is most identified with Wide Right and its sequels when Florida State lost on a missed kick. Bowden claims he wouldn't take back many decisions during his 50-plus years of coaching. He still stands by his decision to keep Mark Richt as offensive coordinator through the 2001 Orange Bowl even though Richt's hiring by Georgia as its head coach caused distractions for Florida State entering that national championship game against Oklahoma. Oklahoma won.

Bowden also remains firm behind his decision to have Gerry Thomas go for a 34-yard field goal on third down with time enough to try one more play before attempting the kick. Thomas missed. Miami won 17-16, and on November 16, 1991, "Wide Right" entered the sports world's vernacular.

Some people might say, "Golly, it wasn't fourth down. Why didn't you throw it into the end zone?" But if you throw it in there and get it intercepted, you kick yourself in the rear the rest of your life. You got a good kicker, so let's go for it. So no, I wouldn't do that any differently.

But Bowden's most memorable Florida State-Miami series is best remembered for a kick that wasn't attempted. Rather than going for a game-tying extra point during the era before overtime, Florida State attempted a two-point conversion that failed. Miami won 26-25. It was the decision to go for two against Miami in 1987 that Bowden would take back today, a rare exception in 50-plus years of coaching.

Right now, I would kick. Back in those days I had never gone for a tie, and I let that get the best of me. If we had kicked, we might have won a national championship. I ain't tying, and I ain't ever going to tie. It was just a macho kind of thing.

Instead, Bowden went for a two-point conversion following an 18-yard touchdown catch by Ronald Lewis with 42 seconds remaining. The pass from Danny McManus to tight end Pat Carter never reached its target—knocked down by Miami's Bubba McDowell. The defeat was the only blemish that season for Florida State, and the Seminoles finished second in the final Associated Press polls. It was Bowden's best finish yet at Florida State, and the highest ranking for a Florida Sate team up to that point, but Miami won the national title.

After the game we went in the locker room, and the first thing I said to the players was, "I apologize to you. We should have kicked."

Carter was among many who wanted nothing to do with it.
"He and Coach McDuffie tried to apologize to us afterwards," he says. "I felt that wasn't necessary."

Bowden admits that sentiment helped.

I felt like I had let them down. And they said, "Oh no, we wanted to go for it." They made me feel a little better.

Just prior to the play, Bowden sent Derek Schmidt to try the extra point. But during a timeout called by Miami, he reconsidered and sent quarterback McManus out for the win.

Sammie Smith, Florida State's fast and powerful tailback, who became a first-round draft choice of the Miami Dolphins, rallied support for the two-point conversion during the timeout.

"I can remember him kind of asking us on the sideline, and Deion [Sanders] and myself standing there and saying— 'Let's go for two points,'" Smith says.

I felt like there was nearly enough time for them to still score. And three yards against them guys is pretty dang tough. So we send the kicking team out there. My thinking was nearly exactly the same thinking I had when we tied Florida 31-31: "This is too great a game to lose. So let's kick it, tie it up, and go from there. Let them gamble."

So I send them out there [for the extra point attempt].

Then Danny McManus was standing there with the most wounded look on his face. "Why aren't we going for a win? Why aren't we going for a win? You're going to kick?"

When he said that, I thought, "Dadgum, these guys want to go after this thing."

Now if they hadn't called time, we would have probably kicked and tied the darn thing. But they called time, and I got to thinking, "My boys want to go for this." So we tried it and missed it.

To this day, Smith insists Bowden did the right thing.

"One of my biggest disappointments professionally or during my collegiate career was that game," he says. "That was the toughest loss I've ever experienced. To be beating a team like we were—19-3 in the third quarter—and the fact we hadn't beat these people for so long, it was really devastating.

"But as a player when you play hard all day long, which we did that day, you don't play for a tie. Yeah, had we played for the tie that game and went on to have the type of season we did the rest of the year, we probably would have won a national championship. But if we had to do it over again, I'd still go for two.

"It showed he had a lot of confidence and trust in our team. He believed in us—that we could get the job done. That decision says a lot about him."

Brad Scott remembers how Bowden's actions also spoke volumes in a subdued coaches meeting after another loss to Miami—a 31-0 dismantling in the 1988 season opener.

"He was as calm as could be, 'I'm disappointed, you're disappointed. I didn't sleep. You didn't sleep,'" Scott recalls. "'Did anybody lose a loved one over the weekend? Men, it's important, but it ain't the most important thing.

"'We're all embarrassed, and we got to do something about it, but let's keep it in perspective. Let's understand there is a lot more to life than just this football game.'

"And boy, that just impressed the heck out of me."

Florida State won the next 11 games after the 1988 season-opening defeat and followed the one-point loss in 1987 with seven consecutive victories.

At Miami, 1992—The "Real" Birth of the Fast-Break Offense

The 1987 meeting may be the most memorable of Bowden's games against Miami, but he says the 19-16 loss to the Hurricanes in 1992 is probably the most important. College football fans remember that game as Wide Right II—kicker Dan Mowrey missed a 39-yard field goal attempt that would have tied the game with no time remaining. Bowden remembers it as the birth of Florida State's no-huddle, shotgun offense—

soon to be known as the "fast-break offense" under the direction of quarterback/point guard Charlie Ward.

The fast-break offense led Florida State to the national championship in 1993 and won Ward the Heisman Trophy the same year.

Bowden says he became interested in the shotgun on visits to see his sons.

Terry was coaching in 1987 at Samford [formerly known as Howard College, where Bowden was a player and coach in the 1950s and 1960s]. Terry always copied everything I did, and Tommy was at Alabama. Tommy was working under Homer Smith, and [Smith] was one of the most brilliant minds on offense I've ever known. So Tommy learned the shotgun, and Terry learned it from Tommy.

Alabama had the shotgun, and Terry had the shotgun, and we didn't. I'd go up there and watch them practice and said, "Dang, we ought to have the shotgun in."

So I would come back to my coaches and do what I usually do—suggest. "Why don't you all do it?" I always liked it to be their idea. They wouldn't do the shotgun. They would never do it. I made them put it in. I do remember that. And so when we started fall practice in 1992, I said, "Now look, if we get in the last minute of a ballgame and we're behind and we got to score, we might as well get in the shotgun. Why get up under the center? You ain't going to run the ball, and they know you aren't going to. Everybody in the stadium knows you're going to throw it. Get back there and start throwing it. I want you to put in a shotgun just for the two-minute offense. Just for the end of the game."

And they were, "OK, we'll do that. We would if we were way behind."

So they did it, and we noticed every time we got in the two-minute offense we scored.

The idea of a fast-break offense apparently took off during the family's annual outing at Panama City.

A family vacation with the Bowdens can be just as productive for grid-iron performance as the "iffy meetings." (Photo courtesy of Bobby Bowden)

"I remember sitting at the beach at Panama City, and Dad talking about it the summer before the '92 season," says Terry, now an analyst with ABC Sports. "Dad ran that split-back, West Coast offense in the mid-'80s up to the early '90s. We're sitting there together in Panama City, and he said, 'You know what I want to do, I want to take the two-minute offense and run it the entire game.

"'If I could do that, I think I can beat anybody and everybody. We got eight plays or eight pass plays and have them all memorized so you're signaling 'em, and we get two deep at every position and run it 60 minutes non-stop.'"

Against Miami, in the fifth game of the 1992 season, Florida State trailed 10-7 in a packed Orange Bowl with 55 seconds remaining before halftime.

They are leading us, and right before the half we go to the shotgun, and Charlie takes them down and scores—we kick a field goal.

Dan Mowrey's 22-yard field goal with 19 seconds left in the first half tied the game. Florida State's success in the shotgun was modest on that drive—the Seminoles collected just 14 yards on six plays.

But with 1:35 left in the game and Florida State trailing 19-16, Ward worked out of the no-huddle, shotgun offense on the final drive. Ward, facing fourth and 12, completed a pass to Kez McCorvey for 25 yards and a first down. Ward kept the ball on the next play and ran for 17 yards after he spotted an inviting hole. He followed that with a 17-yard pass to Matt Frier and then kept the ball again for a two-yard gain before stepping out of bounds at Miami's 22-yard line. Two plays later, Mowrey attempted the field goal. It went wide right, and Florida State lost.

But Bowden liked what he saw before Mowrey's miss. Of course, Florida State had run the two-minute offense prior to that game. But he says the Miami game convinced him to take it up a notch.

I begin to think, "Well, hold on now." We go out and play Miami 60 minutes and can't move the ball worth a darn. We score once, but I don't know how. But right before the half he takes us right down and scores, and then at the end of the game he gives us that chance to tie.

Why don't we use the two-minute offense the whole game—that was my thinking. I might have mentioned it to some other coaches after the game, but I know it was going through my head.

That [Miami game] is where I saw the light—Charlie Ward is better in the shotgun. I first thought Charlie would be much better up under center because I thought he could run better out of it. But when he took the ball out from under center and came back to pass, he would be turning his back to the defense. He couldn't see what was happening down there. But when he was sitting in that shotgun and took the snap, he could see everything. And if a big hole opened right there, boom, he was gone. He couldn't see that coming out of center.

Those thoughts begin to add up.

Brad Scott, Bowden's offensive coordinator, says that he and quarterbacks coach Mark Richt were more sold on the idea than they apparently let on or just more than Bowden realized during the shotgun's infancy in 1992. The two visited the Buffalo Bills and Tampa Bay Buccaneers after that season to perfect the blocking schemes that Scott said concerned Bowden. With four and maybe five receivers spread out, Ward could be an easy target for unaccounted-for defensive players who slipped by Florida State blockers.

"Charlie would say, 'I can make one miss, but I'm having trouble with two,'" Scott says.

The staff's visit to Buffalo provided Florida State with a better idea of how to protect Ward. Florida State coaches also picked up a new play on that trip according to Bowden.

That's where they came up with the play "Direct." Instead of snapping the ball to the quarterback, they snapped it to [Warrick] Dunn. Boy, that was a sweet play. That came from Buffalo. That was a big play for us the next season, in 1993. We ran it first against Miami—we had third and seven, and he got nearly 30 yards.

So in 1993 is when we really perfected that fast-break offense, but it began with Miami and then Georgia Tech the year before.

The Georgia Tech game that came two games after Miami was recognized by the media as the birthplace of the fast-break offense.

"The first time I remember him doing it was against Georgia Tech on TV, and they were down," Terry says. "Most people assume it was that game."

But to Bowden, it remains Miami.

That was the beginning of that thing right there. After Miami we played against North Carolina, and we won it big and probably didn't have to get in the shotgun. But now we go up to Georgia Tech the next week. We're playing conventional offense, and the game gets out of control. I might have said, "Let's get in the shotgun and air it out. It is the only chance we have."

Scott says he and Richt shared Bowden's thinking against Georgia Tech that the no-huddle shotgun was the right move late in the game.

"That's our only chance to win the game," Scott says, "And Coach Bowden said—'Run the dadgum thing and see what happens.'

"After the game he came in the locker room with a big ol' smile and said, 'That thing might have just saved our life.' Then in Monday's staff meeting he said, 'Let's just by golly get into that thing for the whole game and see what happens.'"

Bowden says Ward made this change an easy choice. Ward, who had a penchant for throwing interceptions early in his first season as a starter, threw two of his 17 interceptions that junior year early against Georgia Tech. Florida State trailed early in the fourth quarter 21-7. The Seminoles coaches had tried Danny Kanell at quarterback but without success. He went one for two for seven yards.

We had gotten into a pattern that, when he got into trouble, we'd take him out of the game and put Danny Kanell in. Danny was no more ready to play than the man in the moon. He was a pure freshman, and no way was he ready. We'd just have him run the ball.

Ward's second interception and the second snared by outside linebacker Marlon Williams set up Georgia Tech's second touchdown for an 18-7 lead.

We called a reverse pass and we had the guy open, and Charlie threw it right into the chest of [Williams]. Not here, not there, but right in his chest. And we were wondering why Charlie didn't see him. And that guy takes it all the way down to near their goal line, and they score. And then they get even more ahead of us.

Florida State trailed 21-7 with less than 15 minutes to play and the ball on its 20-yard line.

We were getting beat so bad. We just told Charlie to get in the shotgun. Between running and throwing, he accounted for 207 yards of 208 on our final three scoring drives.

Florida State rallied to a 29-24 victory, and Bowden had confirmation of what he had suspected in Miami two weeks earlier.

Boy, that Charlie was something out of that shotgun.

And the shotgun, according to son Terry, says something about his father as a coach.

"I use it in a lot of my motivational talks," he says. "Here my old man is 63 years old that year, and he's deciding if he can change and do something first before somebody else, he can win a national championship. And it won him a national championship.

"It's the old football saying that the first guy who put the wishbone in won the national championship and the last guy to take it out got fired. Dad was really the first guy to take the shotgun to another level and introduce pace. Pace was the thing that Dad introduced and made the shotgun a little different by going out there in the no-huddle with it. You get into no-huddle, you're taking the defensive coordinator out of the game, at least the first couple of years you did it until they learned to catch up with it.

"That's a great example of a guy who has never been afraid to make a change and wasn't afraid to go out and try something different."

Part IV
Conclusion

Don't Beat Yourself

Bowden has six victories over Nebraska, but he hasn't been so fortunate against another Midwestern powerhouse.

Oklahoma is the answer—twice—to this question to Bowden: Are there Florida State games in which you felt you were outcoached?

The Oklahoma game. I have to say the last one.

In the Bowl Championship Series title game in the 2001 Orange Bowl, Florida State held No. 1 Oklahoma to 13 points, but the Seminoles' offense scored no points. The third-ranked Seminoles came into the game as a 10 1/2-point favorite, but their only points came on a safety.

Without All-America receiver Marvin "Snoop" Minnis— suspended from the game for academic reasons—Florida State collected just 301 total yards of offense, nearly 250 yards under its average during the regular season.

We didn't mix it up good enough. We could have run it more. We just got impatient and went to the throwing game all the way when we were making four of five yards running.

Bowden also points to the 1981 Orange Bowl. Again Oklahoma was the opponent. The Sooners won 18-17 with a two-point conversion with 1:47 remaining.

I don't how they beat us in that Orange Bowl game. I always remember on that last drive of theirs—when they went for two. If I had to do that over, I'd have taken a timeout. They went for two, and we weren't even lined up right.

I'm sure there were several others where we felt we were out-coached.

Howard Schnellenberger was an adversary whom Bowden respected and liked. There was no shame in losing to Schnellenberger, who led Miami to its first national championship in 1983. But Florida State was ranked ninth nationally and a favorite over unranked Miami in 1980 when quarterback Rick Stockstill's two-point conversion pass was deflected. Miami won 10-9. The game featured a controversial call on a long pass from Miami quarterback Jim Kelly that was ruled pass interference at Florida State's one-yard line (in an era when the penalty placed the ball at the point of the infraction).

Howard just did a tremendous job that day. Howard out-coached me. I got too conservative. People wonder about conservatism around here, and they like to blame it on the offensive coordinator. That's usually me. I've been in enough football games to know this is the way you win. This is the way you keep from getting beat.

Those trick plays stand out and give you a reputation of being a gambler. But I still go by that theory that was embedded in me by Bob Neyland and Bear Bryant: The first thing you got to do is not beat yourself. An example was Miami out here in the rain [in 2003]. If we played conservative and punted instead of throwing from our 10-yard line—that they intercepted—that's called beating yourself.

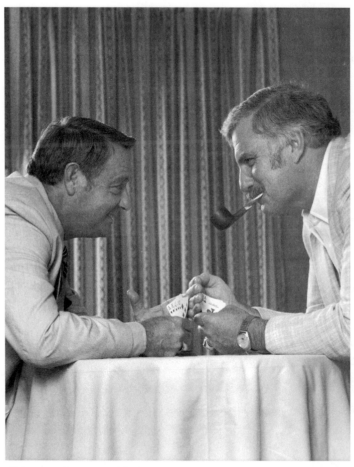

"The Riverboat Gambler" meets his match. Bowden didn't usually come up with aces against friendly adversary Howard Schnellenberger. (Photo courtesy of Bobby Bowden)

Gathering Dust

Out of the games we've played, and I got tapes of all of them, I never go back and look at them. Never. I imagine one of these days when I retire I might enjoy doing [that]. I usually look at them right after we played them, and that's the last time I look at them.

When Bowden finally looks back on his 340 games and counting at Florida State, tapes from games against Miami, Florida, Nebraska, and Notre Dame will fill the screen. But he'll also watch games that have no significant meaning except that they are just fun to watch.

One was a 29-26 victory at Arizona State in 1983 that few Seminoles saw because the night game from Phoenix was not televised. But the game's ending, known as "The Drive," quickly earned a place in Florida State's offensive lore. And Bowden says he'll never forget the game for its sheer excitement. Florida State was ahead 14-13 when starting quarterback Lowrey left the game early in the fourth quarter with a knee injury.

Our quarterback gets knocked out in that game, and we had to go to Bob Davis, a kid from Warner Robins, [Georgia,] whose dad was a high school coach. Now he didn't have that much game experience.

Davis, in fact, had attempted just 11 passes in his collegiate career before that night. And he played that game with one contact lens—the other was accidentally washed down his hotel sink.

That was back when I was calling plays and, on [Davis's fourth play], I called for a pass and he hit it about 40 yards for a touchdown.

I remember when I called it, the coaches were saying, "You better throw something easy, throw something he can complete to give him confidence."

Despite Davis's quick success, Florida State trailed 26-22 with less than two minutes remaining with the ball on its 18-yard line. The first major obstacle in that drive was to overcome a fourth and five on its 23-yard line. Davis hit tight end Tom Wheeler on a drag for 16 yards. Two plays later, Wheeler grabbed a Davis pass and rumbled to the Arizona State 10-yard line.

Davis finished the improbable night when he found Jessie Hester on a square-out pattern in the end zone with six seconds remaining.

A great spectator game.

Chapter 2

Trick Plays

Part I
How It All Started

"Go Down There by the Telephone Pole and Run Back Around"

Bobby Bowden figures that he tried his first trick play in the front yard of his family's three-bedroom house a couple of long passes away from Berry Field in Birmingham, Alabama. Berry Field is where he would play later for Howard College and earn Little All-America honors at quarterback.

It would be one of those—you go down there by the telephone pole and run back around it, or I'll throw it over here to you and you throw back to me. I always played touch out in the yard. I had this football uniform my dad got me—with cardboard shoulder pads and canvas pants. Boy, that was a big deal.

When I about 14 years old, every Sunday we'd get a bunch of guys together and would go play touch football down at the Howard College football field. There was a guy who lived three houses down the street. He was 23 and married. A lot of times I would be the smallest—not so much the youngest but the smallest.

They called them "barnyard plays," and the phrase is still used by Bowden and his assistants. Although Bowden's first house had a chicken yard, it's not where he took the term "barnyard plays" for trick plays.

It's an evil thing. If you got the ball and you ran a trick play on me, you were chicken you-know-what. That's where "barnyard plays" came from.

A young Bobby Bowden (left) designed trick plays in his front yard long before he took them to Doak Campbell Stadium. (Photo courtesy of Bobby Bowden)

Bowden says he never lost the urge to play trickster, especially in his early years at Florida State when "barnyard plays" had an important place in the playbook.

Trick plays allowed the new Florida State head coach to even the playing field against faster, stronger, and better teams in the late 1970s and beyond.

I think a lot of that is the environment in which I was raised. I'm one of those guys who always played with the older guys. I weighed 110 when I went to high school and weighed 116 when I went out for football. When we played touch football, I had to do tricks and stuff like that.

A lot of that comes from being an underdog. When you're favored, you don't need tricks, and that's the way it was when we came here—we were the underdog. I was a tricker in those days.

Of course, I've been in many games where I knew we could lose it, but I never went into a game not trying to win it. I've gone into a game where my thinking is, "We don't have a chance, but I'm going to try to beat him."

You take a gamble. I call a gamble a calculated risk. That's military language. That's General Patton. It's going to be a risk, but it's calculated—it's supposed to work. We've worked on this thing so much. Doing it at the right time is the key.

At Florida State, Bowden mined the state of Florida's deep quarry of blue-chip talent and built a college football dynasty of unparalleled consistency in the late 1980s and through the next decade. As Florida State rang off an NCAA record 14 straight seasons (1987-2000) in the top five of the Associated Press' final poll, the Florida State coach depended less on smoke and mirrors to beat opponents.

Trick plays almost became a thing of the past in the twilight of Bowden's Florida State career. Almost, he says.

You can hardly resist them. We don't run trick plays as much as we used to, but we still got them. We still work on them. A lot of it is we don't need them as much. We have better players than we used to. We have them just for the heck of it. The guys like them. For a receiver to throw a pass is kind of fun.

But you know, we might have as many trick plays as we've ever had. We just don't call them as much. We go into every game with trick plays.

"The Riverboat Gambler" Fools the House

Bowden's penchant for trick plays eventually earned him the nickname "The Riverboat Gambler." But in 1981, he was garnering his first nickname at Florida State: "King of the Road." In a schedule set before he arrived—but heartily embraced by Bowden—Florida State played four major powerhouses on the road in October after already winning at Nebraska in the lone late September game.

With 269 victories at Florida State, Bowden has often left the field atop his players' shoulders. (Photo by Phil Coale/Sunset Images)

The Seminoles upset three of those teams—Ohio State, Notre Dame, and LSU—and lost in a rout to Pittsburgh—in a run that became known as "Octoberfest" and catapulted Florida State into a new level of national recognition.

The season ended weakly, as the Seminoles ran out of gas and lost three straight games. The most humbling was a 58-14 loss to Southern Mississippi, which entered the game 7-0-1. Quarterback Reggie Collier threw for two touchdowns and ran for 150 yards, and the Golden Eagles scored on their first seven possessions. Yet the loss would lead to another Bowden trick play.

That was after Octoberfest, and we were beat to a pulp. The next year we were headed to Southern Mississippi. And our defensive coaches said, "We ain't going to let that quarterback beat us."

Our whole defense was [saying], "We're going to get that quarterback." And boy, we did. But the tailback [Sam Dejarnette], whom we hadn't heard anything about, got a little over 300 yards rushing.

We're doing pretty good, and we were tied up 17-17 with about five minutes left in the game.

Quarterback Kelly Lowrey took his team to the Golden Eagles' two-yard line, where Bowden faced an easy fourth-down decision.

All you got to do is kick a field goal, and you're ahead of them 20-17. But I remember my thinking, and I expressed it to George Henshaw, my offensive coordinator, "If they get the ball back, they'll drive down and get a field goal. We ain't stopping them. We can slow them down, but we have hardly been able to stop their guys, and they have plenty of time to kick a field goal."

Well, George had worked all week on a fake field goal he felt would work on them after watching the film. So I say, "Let's do it. Let's go for it." Well, they know it's going to be a field goal because three points win the game. We snap the ball to Kelly Lowrey [who was in to hold the snap], and he picks up the ball and goes in standing up. Sure enough, they take the ball all the way back to nearly the 25-yard line, where they could have kicked a field goal for the tie if we hadn't run the trick play.

That was one of the most successful trick plays, and one you don't hear people talking about too much.

And I would have to say it was the gutsiest call.

Here, we had a field goal that would put us ahead. It's not like so many games, like the Puntrooskie, that we were in the position we almost had to gamble. But here we had the ball on the four-yard line and an easy field goal. Why would we pass it up? But I felt like their quarterback could come back and set up a field goal. Henshaw put that in. I called it, but he was the one who saw it. And sure enough, they came back and were in field goal range.

A Reversal of Fortune

In the 28 years I've been here, let's say we've had 50 reverses. Well, you can bet your life I called it 49 times. I have been vetoed [over the years] when I call it, and it makes me so mad I can hardly stand it.

What I do a lot of times is say, "Run this play." They'll say, "No, it's not good. They got an end over there watching for it." If I really like it, I say, "Run it." And they run it.

By the time Bowden secured his reputation as "The Riverboat Gambler," the reverse had become standard fare. It remains a Bowden favorite.

When Bowden calls the reverse, it can be the cause for nervous moments in the coaches' box. Bowden runs the play so often, it's hardly a trick or a surprise to opponents. But even when Bowden's assistants know it will fail and the opponent sees it is coming, the reverse can still be Bowden's best friend. That was the case in the season opener of 1999, Florida State's second national championship season.

The game against Louisiana Tech was tied at 7-7 late in the first half when a frustrated Bowden took the offense out of the hands of coordinator Mark Richt.

"We were stumbling around," assistant coach John Lilly says. "We weren't exactly looking like the No. 1 team in America. And Coach Bowden said, 'Look, I'm going to call the plays.'"

I used to call the plays when I first got here. But in recent years, only occasionally I'll take over a series. Usually, it's just for fun. But in that situation I must have seen something. If I thought I had the answer, I'd take over. I have that right. I keep that policy. I have final veto.

And predictably, Bowden immediately called a reverse. Peter Warrick ran it for 21 yards and a first down on a third-

and-two situation. Anquan Boldin followed two plays later with a reverse for 13 yards. A 33-yard pass to Talman Gardner put Florida State at Louisiana Tech's 20-yard line with under a minute remaining in the first half.

"In the coaches' box I'm the guy who Coach Bowden always tells to, 'Check if the reverse is [possible],'" Lilly says. "By then you're saying, 'Boy, the reverse isn't going to work again.'

"Well, Coach Richt taught me to just tell Coach it is there because he's going to call it anyway. You knew he was in the mood for it, so you're not going to say anything.

"So Coach Bowden calls that third reverse, and you know they are going to be waiting over there. And sure enough, they were. But of course, it set up Pete and the play of the year."

When Warrick took the pitch from quarterback Chris Weinke, he ran to his right, where he found Tech defensive players waiting. He went back to his left and began a ball-juggling, tackle-dodging odyssey that seemingly took him through several time zones before he finished in the end zone with a 20-yard touchdown.

Bowden still chuckles when he thinks of the play's success.

They had it defended. A guy was waiting for it, and he turned the other way. That's the most memorable one—that play. Peter did exactly what I told him to do.

Bowden laughs.

He made that work by himself.

The play was an instant hit on ESPN's *SportsCenter* and later was featured in the College Hall of Fame as one of college football's all-time greatest plays. Bowden made it even more legendary during his Monday luncheon when he provided the following play-by-play:

"Now you saw me talking to him before he went in. I had to explain it to him. He had a hard time understanding, boy, all

Bowden is the architect and executor of some of the best trick plays in college football. (Photo by Phil Coale/Sunset Images)

I wanted him to do. Now you get over to the left, and you get the ball and run it around the right side. Now when you get over there, the defensive end—you've already run that thing once—he's looking for it. He's going to try and contain you.

"When he does, you start it back up the middle. There will be two big ol' boys there. ... So cut back to the left. And get here in haste. But you get over here, a guy is going to unload on you and about knock your britches off. Kick your leg up high and shove off the other way, and you can escape him. And by doing that, you make the rest of the guys think you're down.

"Come back down on your feet and continue running to your left.

"They're going to see what happened, so I want you to fool them. Throw the ball up. Run without the ball. When it comes down, you'll see this guy here noticing. So turn around and go back the other way. You were just down this way not long ago. Now ol' No. 37 is going to throw a block on this guy, and sooner or later, you've got to head to towards their goal line, so go. ... There'll be two guys there. Hang a right..."

Bowden had the fans rolling in the aisles. But he had already elicited the biggest chuckles from his staff.

"We always laugh—if any of us were to have suggested that play, it would have gotten thrown for a 15-yard loss," Lilly says. "But since Coach Bowden called it, it goes for a touchdown and is the play of the year in college football."

Then-offensive coordinator Mark Richt said Bowden was anything but lucky on that play.

"He was smart on that because he knew to get the ball to Peter," said Richt, now the head coach at Georgia. "He did a lot better job of that than I did. He was always thinking in terms of getting the play to this particular guy. And I was more inclined to get more than one player in the picture and let the quarterback decide who should get the ball according to what the defense was doing. Any given play when I called it could go to one of any three guys depending on the defense. Coach was more apt to get Peter Warrick or so-and-so the ball.

"Where I learned that lesson [about utilizing playmakers better] was the national championship game against Tennessee [in the 1999 Fiesta Bowl that was won by the Vols]. Warrick touched the ball just once or twice, and when that game was over, I thought what I was doing was good systematically, but I also had to make sure I had a little box on my call sheet to make sure this kid got the ball more in his hand."

Bowden says Peter Warrick was too good to ignore.

I would make them show me going into a game how many ways you got to get the ball into Peter Warrick's hand where he is the primary receiver. Not might get it to him, but where he is the primary receiver. List as many ways as you can to put the ball in his hand as a playmaker. That's something they did a really good job in that national championship game, where we won it over Virginia Tech. We won the national championship doing that.

Borrowing, Not Stealing

I've always liked the reverse. Always liked it.

To me it's a play that really helps keep a defense honest. If the ball goes this way, and they all run it over there and smear it, you can't block 'em all. But when they run over there, and then you run a reverse back over here, it's got a chance to come out there pretty good. We run it so much now, they are looking for it.

But I'm still looking for it. I'll tell John Lilly going into a game, "Johnny, watch that backside end. Let me know if he ain't paying attention for the reverse."

Bowden says he introduced Florida State to the reverse in 1977—his second season as the Seminoles' head coach. A dozen seasons had passed since he watched Virginia Tech burn Florida State on a pair of fumblerooskies, and in 1977 he was on the receiving end of another Tech trick. Virginia Tech tight end Mickey Fitzgerald, whom Bowden remembers as being about 260 pounds, was moved to fullback for one purpose.

"They ran the trap on us, and I mean they ran the trap to death," then-defensive assistant Jim Gladden says. "We were not prepared for it and could not stop it. You had [linebackers] Aaron Carter and Jimmy Heggins [current Florida State offensive line coach] trying to stop a 260-pound fullback on the trap. We would hit him, and he'd drag us for five or six."

Bowden's response was to feature Mike Shumann in the reverse three times against the Hokies. On one reverse, the left-handed Shumann threw a pass to Roger Overby that set up the winning field goal with under five minutes to play.

The two players Bowden believes executed the reverse the best don't include Warrick, although Warrick's reverse against Louisiana Tech is the most revered among Florida State fans.

Lawrence Dawsey wasn't real fast, but he could run the reverse. The way he'd run it, if they had it stopped, he'd cut back in

Bowden calls the shots during his first couple of seasons coaching at Florida State. (Photo courtesy of Bobby Bowden)

here and make yardage. And of course Darrin Holloman, gosh, he was good at running it.

Bowden allows the reverse nearly was omitted from his playlist early in his coaching career. He said the first time he ran it, as the head coach at West Virginia, it lost 17 yards against Pittsburgh.

That broke me for a long time of running the reverse.

The reverse is the most used of all trick plays by Bowden at Florida State. It is also symbolic of a philosophy that was fundamental in Bowden becoming Division I-A's all-time winningest coach in 2003.

I like to call it borrowing. Not stealing. Borrowing. If this play or this formation or defense worked for somebody else—won them a national title, then maybe it can work for us. We've done that not just with trick plays.

I see it and I like it and say, "Why don't we try it?" I'll take anything I see that's good. I'm not proud. And I'll give them credit for it. I think most trick plays that people use, they saw somebody else do it. And you know where you get most of them trick plays? Out of high school, because they'll try anything. I have had a lot of good ideas come from high school coaches.

I've had people send me trick plays. I usually look at them, but we never used them. Most of them just aren't sound. No way they worked, but later after we've run our own trick play, they might write me back and say, "I'm glad you used my play." A coach may write me, and I may try it.

Now I'll come up with an idea and our coaches will come up with a lot of things just by studying film. Noticing that a safety sets up here, and maybe we can do this. But I'm not afraid to borrow.

Many other trick plays in addition to the reverse were successfully run against Bowden and then stored away for a later

Bowden cuts the cake after getting his 100th win. He would go on to become the NCAA's all-time winningest coach in 2003. (Photo courtesy of Bobby Bowden)

day and possibly more tweaking. The Puntrooskie, the trick play most associated with Bowden, is the best example of that.

The first time I ever saw it was in 1965 out here [in Doak Campbell Stadium]. I was an assistant coach, and we were playing Virginia Tech, and Jerry Claiborne was their head coach. He ran it on us that night twice. Twice. Not for a touchdown but for long gains. That caught my attention. I said, "Good gracious, the fact they could run it on us twice, that's a heck of a play."

Bowden filed the play away and finally used it at the end of the 1972 season. He was West Virginia's head coach by then, and the Mountaineers were preparing for Lou Holtz and North Carolina State in the Peach Bowl.

I called Jerry Claiborne and got him to tell me exactly how he ran it. I put it in as running play instead of a punt. I had the quar-

terback hide the ball behind his leg for a back hiding up there, and we ran it for 14 yards. That was the first time I ever ran it.

The Puntrooskie

Sixteen years later, Bowden ran it as a fake punt—the Puntrooskie—in what then-ESPN analyst Beano Cook called "the greatest play since *My Fair Lady*."

Peter Warrick's razzle-dazzle reverse may have zig-zagged its way to the College Hall of Fame and that fake punt against Southern Mississippi in 1982 found its way to Bowden's heart, but the Puntrooskie is *the* trick play.

That's the play you're identified with. We got that term "rooskie" from Tom Osborne and Nebraska—they had the fumblerooskie. Anytime we use the term "rooskie" that means a trick play. And, of course, I had remembered Jerry Claiborne running a variation of the Puntrooskie. The Puntrooskie was very risky. Scary. If it don't work, baby, you're hung in effigy.

The Puntrooskie wasn't even my play, and Wayne McDuffie was the one that made it work in practice. I called it. That one nearly had to come from the head coach. Because if it failed—

Florida State and Clemson were tied 21-21 with the Seminoles at their own 21-yard line with 1:31 remaining. Deep in its own territory and facing fourth and four, Florida State set up for a punt.

LeRoy Butler, the play's main character, remembers the concise words of Coach Bowden as he ran on to the field—"Do it."

"And I'm like, 'We're at around the 20-yard line. We're going to do this play. Are you kidding?'" Butler says.

Bowden, with a laugh, remembers feeling all alone.

I made the call, and there wasn't anybody around. One of the coaches was hiding under the bench, and two went inside.

Can you imagine if the play doesn't work at our 21-yard line?

Something I've done in the past, I say, "Boys, you can call [any rooskie] a 'Bowdenrooskie' if you want to. So if it fails, I get all the blame and not y'all." If it's a rookie, it's usually something I put in. And sometimes the coaches don't want anything to do with it. I mean nothing to do with it.

The Puntrooskie was a product of a lot of borrowing.

In 1988, at the start of the season, Mickey [Andrews] was working on his punt rush and punt block. Clint Ledbetter, he was a graduate assistant for us, was working with the scout squad. And Mickey said to put some trick plays in to see how our kids respond to them. Clint put that play in because he used to run it when he was at Arkansas State. The first time the scout team ran it, it went waaay down there. It worked for about 50 yards. Then later on, Clint ran it again, and it broke again. So when it went twice against our defense, I was thinking that thing must be pretty good.

Bowden asked Ledbetter to get Arkansas State coaches to send footage of the Puntrooskie—a play they had run four times. Then-offensive line coach Brad Scott said he also ran across the play while recruiting in South Georgia and had the play drawn for him on a high school game program.

"We watched it on film—that [Arkansas State] team ran it twice in one game, and it worked both times," former Florida State quarterback Casey Weldon says. "We just laughed and laughed."

Yet Florida State players weren't sure what to make of the play, even after they watched it succeed on the practice field and on film.

"We really didn't know if it was going to work or not," recalls Butler, who became an All-America defensive back and All-Pro with the Green Bay Packers but may be better known for his role in the Puntrooskie. "When we executed it in practice, it really didn't look all that good.

"He always told us he would give us every chance to win. He always made sure he had something special. That's what I love about Coach Bowden is that he gives his players a chance to be great—to be a man—then it's up to you."

Bowden says the plan was to put the Puntrooskie in against Miami in the season opener. Florida State entered the game No. 1 for the first time in school history and was promptly spanked 31-0.

We got beat so bad we would have wasted it. Well, we worked on it after that just in case. Two weeks later we go up there against Clemson, and it was a good time for it to go.

It almost didn't though—at least not in dramatic fashion with 1:31 left in the game. Brad Scott recalls that Bowden considered running it earlier—probably in the first quarter but was talked out of it. With the ball in Clemson territory, the coaches were worried that the Tigers might try to block the punt and that would foil the fake. Florida State punted from the 46-yard line with under three minutes remaining in the first quarter.

Offensive coordinator Wayne McDuffie called for Florida State to run the play late in the first half. Florida State faced a fourth-down situation from its 31-yard line with under a minute remaining in the first half.

Linebackers coach Wally Burnham was sitting next to McDuffie in the coaches' box. "He really wanted to run the play at that point," Burnham says.

Bowden recalls having one response.

"No. No. We're going to save it."
I can remember exactly what my thinking was. They had us 14-7 with a couple of minutes before the half. We had the ball around maybe the 50-yard line, fourth down and something, and that would be the ideal time to do it because you're backed up,

where if you miss it, they still have to go 50 [yards]. Wayne was wanting to do it right then, saying this is a good time for the fake punt.

But this is how confident I was. I said, "No, it will score, and the score will be 14-14, and they'll go into the half mad. It will be better off if they go in ahead and they'll get overconfident. And this way, we can go in and get all over the kids."

The other thing, most trick plays are a desperation thing, and you are beat unless something happens. So it's late in the game when you finally decide to do it. I felt like if we ever ran it, it would work. The reason I was so confident goes back to that we worked it against our defense all the time. So I did feel confident.

But if you do it early in the game, you showed your hand and it's all gone. So I wouldn't let [McDuffie] run it.

Clemson coaches later said they were expecting Florida State to try the play in the first half.

And Bowden used the Puntrooskie at halftime to rally his team.

"Coach Bowden is—'Men, keep your head up, keep your head up,'" Scott says. "'We got the Puntrooskie. We got the Puntrooskie. It's a guaranteed tie because we got the Puntrooskie.' It was like new energy in the locker room when he said that.

"The boys are like, 'Yeah, yeah, we got the Puntrooskie.' Then he calls it at the end of the game, and I remember when he called it—it was like nobody on the staff was even mentioning the Puntrooskie at that point. It was like, 'No way. If we don't get the ball out of here, it's over.'

"I'm thinking—you got to be kidding."

Later, Bowden told his sons at one of their annual get-aways at Panama City that it was the only call to make.

"FSU was 1-1 coming into that game, and they were trailing," Terry Bowden says. "They had to win the game. A tie would ruin the season, too. I remember Dad said, 'We ran that play because it was the only one we could.' They had to be thinking that it was absolutely a ridiculous time to run it. 'No way he would run it then.'"

But he did.

Fullback Dayne Williams, lined up behind the center as a blocker, took the snap instead of punter Tim Corlew and put the ball between his legs. Butler, another upback, pulled out the ball and ran 78 yards before running out of gas and getting pushed out of bounds at the one-yard line. Florida State kicked a 19-yard field goal to win the game 24-21 in the final half-minute.

Gym Plays

Trick plays are a big part of the Bowden legacy, but as the legacy shows, Bowden encourages his offensive staff to dabble in trick plays.

When Chris Weinke faked a tailback dive to Jeff Chaney and with his right shoe near the back of the end zone connected with Marvin "Snoop" Minnis for a 98-yard touchdown against Clemson in 2000—that wasn't Bowden's ace.

Mark Richt called that one—all I did was watch.

Bowden, says Richt, gets more credit than that for the play that Richt first saw as a graduate assistant at Florida State in 1985.

"I'm still using things I learned from Coach Bowden," said Richt, Georgia's head coach since 2001. "That rooskie play we hit Marvin Minnis for 98 yards against Clemson, he used that that against Auburn in 1985 with Eric Thomas. And then when I was out at East Carolina, it won a game for East Carolina, and I've called it three times at Georgia. Two were touchdowns, and one was a very long one for about 50 yards against Tech. If the

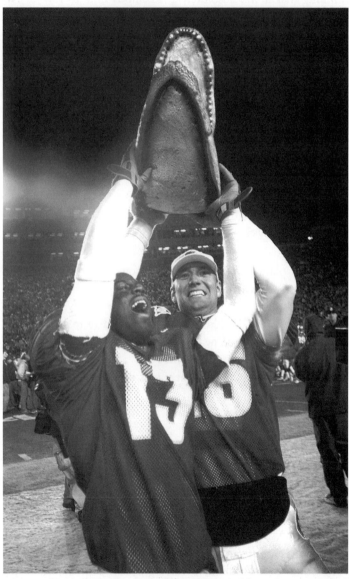

Marvin "Snoop" Minnis and Chris Weinke hold up the Gator head after a win against Florida in 2000. (Photo by Phil Coale/Sunset Images)

kid had thrown it a little farther, it would have been for a touchdown, too."

And Bowden, after it worked, gave trick plays at Florida State yet another name—"gym plays"—because that's where the Weinke-to-Minnis play was practiced.

"We said, 'We'll run this play if we are inside our own five-yard line,'" Weinke says. "'Other than that, we won't run it.' We were at the two-yard line. We put the play in, and I think we maybe practiced it one time—inside."

With a low ceiling on the athletic center practice gym, Weinke was unable to air out the pass as he did in the game. But Weinke and company had seen enough on film to know it would work. Richt borrowed from Bowden's old play by having Weinke completely turn his back to the Clemson defense and then quickly turn and hit Minnis.

"That was a play from [Richt] watching film. We knew when we got in a certain formation, they were a hundred percent in that particular defense," Weinke says. "When we were in a two tight-end set, and the receiver motioned down, we saw what they did.

"And what they did is brought everybody down in the box. We couldn't really practice it. But we knew from watching film it was one of those things where it would be a safety or a touchdown.

"I knew when we started to motion the guy—before I got the snap—it would be a touchdown because they did exactly what we thought they would do."

And Florida State did exactly what Clemson didn't expect.

Bowden also credits Richt for putting receiver Peter Warrick at quarterback—a ploy that paid dividends on several occasions. Warrick kept the ball when he lined up in the shotgun against Georgia Tech in 1999 and ran for a touchdown. Three games later against Duke, Warrick threw a touchdown pass to Laveranues Coles for a 35-yard touchdown.

Peter Warrick at quarterback—that was their thing—Mark and them. I think I might have suggested the pass that Peter

Warrick hit Coles with—"*Y'all should throw a pass off that thing. Let him throw the ball, so they know he won't run it every time he is back there.*"

Those are ones the offensive staff put in. When we're planning for the game, a lot of times they want to do something I might really give the other side of it—*why you shouldn't do it. I'll do that a lot now. I do that knowing that if they are strong enough to stay behind it, they must be right. If I keep saying why do you want to do this, and if this happens, and I don't think it's a good idea, and they come back and say, "Coach, we still think we ought to do it," I usually go along with them.*

Now if they cave in, it means they weren't that strong for that.

During the game, I usually tell them to run a trick play by me first. We go into every game usually with a fake or a trick play. But I tell the coaches, "Now look, don't call it until you check with me." Sometimes they might not run it by me, but I sure want them to. That play Mark put in against Clemson for 98 yards, I didn't even know they called it. I don't even remember working on it. He just put it in, and it worked. I don't want them to be afraid to try stuff. I like it when they do.

The thing I don't want them to do is do it at the wrong time. Against Nebraska in the game we won the national championship, [they] called a pass with the quarterback running to the left and throwing back to William Floyd right down on their 20-yard line, and they [nearly] intercepted it. I didn't want to do that, boy. We were fixin' to kick a field goal. He threw that before [they] even thought about it, and I didn't have time to debate and say, "Don't do it."

Richt said the first time his attempt at a trick play displeased Bowden came the previous year.

"I remember the first reverse I called on my own—it didn't work a hoot, and Coach Bowden made some kind of comment—'I'm in charge of calling those,'" Richt said. "I don't know if it was serious jab or a fun jab. I couldn't tell. But I kind of thought it was his department. In time, we did more. We were on the lookout for them."

Part II
Rival Trickery

More Than a Minor Adjustment

Ten years after the Puntrooskie, Peter Warrick was the key element in a trick play—a pass off a reverse—against the Florida Gators in 1998. Bowden ranks it among his favorite trick plays at Florida State.

We just were in the fourth quarter. Neither one of us were getting a lot done on offense. And you were thinking if you could get a lead, your defense might just hold it. We call a toss sweep, and Travis Minor goes for a touchdown, but it's called back. A penalty. Gosh, we knew we had 'em, and then all of a sudden there's that dadgum flag.

They might be looking for the sweep again. My thinking was that the [Florida] defensive coordinator has got to be saying, "They are coming back with it, and we'll have a defense for it."

And you figure it being so late in the game and with it so tight, they ain't going to be looking for that [reverse pass]. Again, the timing's so important to making these plays go.

That's the most successful trick play we ran recently.

The Seminoles were ahead 13-12 early in the fourth quarter, when, with less than 14 minutes left in the game, tailback Travis Minor broke loose for a 48-yard touchdown on a toss sweep. One problem. Minor benefited from the wrong kind of help, and a holding penalty on Warrick made it first and eight from Florida's 46-yard line. And Bowden was back to the drawing board.

With starting quarterback Chris Weinke unavailable because of a ruptured disc and a chipped vertebra he suffered two games earlier and seldom-used Marcus Outzen in at quarterback, Bowden notes that he was tempted to reach a little deeper into his bag of tricks. The underdog element.

"Coach called [it]," tight ends and recruiting coach John Lilly explains. "We had just run a sweep with Minor that was called back. It was disconcerting to everybody. We had that touchdown. There was such a high, and then you saw that [penalty] flag out there. You have a tendency to come unraveled, and the kids were a little shaky at that point. I remember Coach [Mark] Richt, who is always really calm, saying, 'Look, we need to take a timeout. We need to calm everybody down and get over that.'"

"48Z Reverse Pass" came the call, and during the timeout some coaches admitted they privately questioned the logic of the play.

"We're like, 'Are sure you want that right now?'" Lilly recalls. "'Of course,' came the reply from Bowden.

"And, of course, it worked."

Bowden remembers having no qualms or hesitation about calling the play. He says it wasn't a psychological ploy to rally his troops as some assistants believed at the time. It was strictly a strategic hunch. A gamble. A calculated risk.

His coaches were not as convinced that a pass off the reverse was such a good idea. Jeff Chaney would take the pitch from Outzen and in turn would give the football to Warrick.

"Our defense was playing so well," Lilly says of a unit that held Florida to 204 total offensive yards. "At that point, if we don't give them one, they cannot score and beat us. And obviously, if you run a reverse, you can have a fumbled exchange that puts them right back in the game.

"And the other part of that story is that Travis had just run the sweep, so he was tired. He would usually be in for that play. Coach [Billy] Sexton put Jeff Chaney in, and Jeff that year had a hard time catching the pitch on a sweep. He's not the guy you want catching it, much less catching it and handing it off. We are in such a kind of shock that we're going to run the play—I don't think any of us looked to see who was out there except to make sure Pete was out there."

Of course, Sexton had.

"That's the thing I remember most," Sexton says. "All of a sudden it hits me, 'Oh, no, Chaney is in the game.'"

What began as a simple reverse turned into something more dangerous for Florida and more memorable for Bowden. After taking the ball from Chaney, Warrick drew upon his experience as a quarterback at Bradenton Southeast High School and threw a strike to Ron Dugans for a touchdown and a lead Florida State never surrendered. A year after trying it against Clemson only to see Warrick's pass sail over Dugans, Warrick made it work this time. The 23-12 victory catapulted Florida State into the Bowl Championship Series national title game against Tennessee in the Fiesta Bowl.

"After the game he gave me credit for it, but he did call that one," Richt said.

Turning a Gator into a Crocodile

Two more trick plays Bowden says he cherishes to this day came in one scoring drive at Michigan in 1991 that was part of the fun Florida State had in the 51-31 victory. And for that, he can thank Steve Spurrier, of all people.

We had a 7-0 lead after Terrell Buckley had intercepted a pass and scored a touchdown [on a 40-yard return]. Then after they score, we get down to the 11-yard line on that Casey-to-Charlie-to-Casey play. We can't do anything with the ball, and we come up with a fourth-and-four. We fake the field goal and throw a little underneath pass to [William] Floyd for the touchdown.

What's interesting about it is that not only did we run two tricks plays on one drive, but also it came in the first quarter. Again, a lot of trick plays usually are set up to come later in the game.

Future NFL starting quarterback Brad Johnson was the holder who flicked a shovel pass to Floyd. That trick was set up by quarterback Casey Weldon's long lateral to Charlie Ward, who threw it back to Weldon, who then scampered 29 yards to the Wolverines' 11-yard line. Three plays later, with the ball at the four-yard line, Florida State faked the field goal.

"We only worked on it that week. If we had had more speed back there, we might have scored," Weldon says and laughs. "The thing about Coach Bowden and trick plays [is] it's not just a trick play to have fun. It keeps defenses honest and makes them practice for them.

"Even more than that, it's a game changer. A momentum changer."

Bowden recalls running the throwback again in 1998 against Florida without success, with Peter Warrick and Marcus Outzen as the principals. Outzen dropped the second pass.

That play came from Steve Spurrier. Steve did that out here [in Doak Campbell Stadium] against us the year before [1990], and I said, "Boy, that is a clever play." It didn't work, but I liked it. He was the first one I had seen do it, and a lot of people copied it. It was Steve Spurrier's play, but we named the play "Crocodile." We wouldn't name it "Gator." A Florida State team can't run a play named "Gator."

I say that, but we did have a play called Gator Pass. But it wasn't named after them. It was named because we were going to run it against Florida. If I mention Gator Pass today, every player would know it. We ran it in '84 and ran it against LSU. We ran it against Florida, but I don't remember doing anything big. Terry, in his second year at Auburn [in 1994], hurt Florida bad with the Gator Pass. Florida was No. 1 in the nation, and he beat them down there, and he ran the Gator Pass against them several times and beat them with it.

But that was a play we came up with. The Crocodile was all Steve's.

I used to call Steve when he was at Duke, because maybe I had watched his team on television and saw something. I'd ask him how he did a couple of these things, and he would give them to me. "I saw your game last night and the way you hit your fullback. How did you do that?"

Once he went down there [to Gainesville], the iron curtain dropped on all of that [cooperation].

The other strained relationship between Bowden and a Florida coach involved Charley Pell, who took Florida from an 0-10-1 season in 1979 to three consecutive victories over Florida State before he was forced to step down three games into the 1984 season at a time when the school was under NCAA scrutiny. The Bowden and Pell rivalry was not a friendly one, but according to Bowden the two made peace before Pell's death in June 2001.

I called Charley the week before he died. I have no grudges there either. He had cancer. I told him, "I am sorry, and I will be thinking about you and praying for you."

A Tough One to Fool

When we tried trick plays against Miami with Butch Davis back down there, our tricks plays didn't work very good. One time he told me—"We checked all of the film we had on you for 15 years just to get all of your trick plays and work on them. So we were ready for them."

While Davis put a stop to most tricks plays during his six-year stint as Miami's head coach from 1995 through 2000, he saw enough of them as an assistant coach with the Hurricanes from 1984 to 1988. In 1984, Florida State beat Miami thanks to a trick play: a rare reverse off an option. It was a play that new quarterbacks coach Art Baker, a master of the option, brought with him to Tallahassee from East Carolina.

It looks like Eric Thomas is pitching to his pitchman, but it was really to Jessie Hester, who comes all the way from the other way. He goes 77 yards for a touchdown.

The next year, Florida State ran a fake punt that Cletis Jones turned into a 30-yard gain in Florida State's 35-27 defeat to Miami.

Then in 1986, Florida State was down 14-7 to No. 1 Miami when Bowden gave a national television audience another taste of his trickery.

The Hurricanes had just scored on Vinny Testaverde's touchdown pass to Alonzo Highsmith when Florida State returner Keith Ross settled under the kickoff about six yards deep in his end zone. He gave fellow returner Dexter Carter the signal that the trick play was on. Florida State coaches held their breath as Ross bobbled the football—which was not planned—and then dashed to the 15-yard line, where he was surrounded by a half-dozen Hurricanes. Ross, who played two years of minor league baseball before joining the Florida State team, stopped and skipped a lateral across the field to Carter.

Carter, one of Florida State's fastest running backs of all time, caught the lateral at the 10-yard line and ran 90 yards for a touchdown.

"Me and Dexter were given that opportunity to make that decision solely on our own," Ross says. "I'd just signal Dexter. Nobody else knew it was ready to happen. Our upback guys knew of the play, but they didn't know exactly when we were going to do it. The more they were surprised, the better they would sell it."

It wouldn't be the only time that Florida State players were allowed some freedom in tricking the opponent. Three years later, freshman Terrell Buckley pretended to call a fair catch on a punt against Syracuse—and then returned it 69 yards for a touchdown. Later, it was rumored that Bowden was upset with Buckley—a Mississippi native whose play earned him the nickname "The Foola from Pascagoula"—because not only did the coaches not call the play, they weren't aware it was coming.

But Bowden says he wasn't upset with Buckley.

Not at all. That was some play. I wish I had thought of it.

You can have plays where it's up to the player. We've had faked punts out here that were called, and the guy gets up there and sees it won't work and calls it off. Throwbacks on kickoffs, where if the [returner] sees he's got the lateral covered he has to take off. Last season [2003] we had that. Ernie Sims was the upback, and if they do a certain defense, it's not good, and he calls the fake punt off. [Assistant coach] Jody Allen would have to clear it through me before he could call the fake punt. But we had it on several times where it was what we wanted to do, but the upback called it off. That's a very big decision they have to make.

Ross says that plays such as that and the one he and Carter executed are a testimony to Bowden's trust in his players.

"A coach has to have faith in your players, and you in your coach," Ross says. "If I know that Coach has enough trust and faith in me to get a play like that done, it's just going to help me play better."

That faith in his players paid off with a play that not even the Miami staff quickly forgot—Ross's toss to Carter.

"Historically they've always had a variety of things," says Cleveland Browns coach Davis, a defensive line coach on Jimmy Johnson's 1986 Miami staff. "It's just part of the preparation to get your team to be alert and aware. The one that probably stands out the most is the throwback on the kickoff that went for a touchdown against us [in 1986] in the Orange Bowl."

T.K.'s Play

The Miami staff would have needed to go back farther than 15 years to find the basis for the Ross-Carter trick toss.

Bowden calls it "T.K.'s play" after T.K. Wetherell, the current Florida State president, who made the play work as a football receiver in 1965. Bowden, then an assistant, was Wetherell's coach. And Bowden and assistant Bobby Jackson devised the play, according to Wetherell.

Wetherell and Bill Moreman combined for a 100-yard kickoff return against Kentucky. Moreman settled under the kickoff in the end zone. He ran out before throwing it laterally to Wetherell, who caught the football at the 13-yard line and ran 87 yards to the other end zone. The play worked against Miami, and it failed against Syracuse in 1966.

Wetherell says that Bowden's trick plays under Coach Bill Peterson were revealing in a number of ways.

"Most of the trick plays Bobby runs are in the second half," he says. "That's by design. Set the play up. The kickoff throw against Kentucky, we had scored and then Kentucky scored twice in response. They were all fired up, and they come down the field all excited. They don't stay in their lanes, and we exploit that.

"Bowden had some weird stuff during that time when he was an assistant—stuff he drew in dirt sometimes. He even had a reverse using a tackle. But it all had a couple of purposes. We didn't have the talent level others had, so we had to make it up with speed and ingenuity. Line up and play them straight, and you'd get killed.

"And we ran the trick plays at the end of practice. Instead of wind sprints, we ran trick plays, so you had a way of conditioning that was fun."

And as with so many plays, especially the ones that worked, Bowden made a mental note of Wetherell's touchdown against Kentucky.

I do not have a book of trick plays. No notebook. I just keep them in my head.

Although Wetherell's play has resurfaced, Bowden says a change in the rules makes it difficult to execute with the same effectiveness.

They've changed the blocking rules, and you don't see it as much as you used to. It's not as good with the rule change. You used to block below the body—throw your body. When you throw your body, nobody hardly misses and you put the opponent down. If you do miss the block, they at least have to jump over you and around you, and that slows them down.

A Non-trick That Tricks Miami

Against stingy Miami, Bowden has learned to appreciate the gamble that pays off—even when it's not a trick play. A screen pass isn't considered a trick play by most coaches, but Bobby Bowden points to one as a memorable gamble that paid off against Miami in his third season with the Seminoles. Florida State was ahead 24-21 in the fourth quarter.

[Mark] Lyles was the fullback. We got down to their 22-yard line, and it's fourth down and maybe one or two. We were out of field goal range, but somehow we needed to score. I called a screen pass, and Wally Woodham was the quarterback. And the coaches were screaming like mad—"Don't run the screen! Don't run the screen! If they intercept the ball, they can beat us."

So we ran it, and Wally hits Lyles, and he ran it [22 yards] for a touchdown. Afterwards, the coaches kidded me about it—"That was a great call."

That wasn't a play many Seminoles fans likely remember, or have even heard of, but it underscores Bowden's philosophy about taking chances.

The key to trick plays is to call them at the right time. I've seen people who have had great trick plays but called them at a time when it can't work.

Part III
Tricking the Trickster

A Rooskie to Forget

Then there are the trick plays Bowden wishes he couldn't remember.

We had a couple of different rooskies. Of course, the Puntrooskie is one everybody remembers. And we had the Guardrooskie against Auburn [in 1990] that cost us a touchdown. I wish I hadn't done that. That's one where they kicked a field goal in the last second and beat us after the Guardrooskie failed. We lost 20-17.

We were tied 17-17. We were driving, and we were down at about their 40-yard line. We had a third down and long [17 yards], and we tried that dadgum play. The idea was for Casey Weldon to take the snap, and he lays the ball on the ground behind his legs. One of our guards [Mike Morris] would pick it up and run with it, and they usually don't ever see it because everybody is running the other way. They knew we had it—they were looking for it, and when we did it, they went and got the ball. When our center laid the ball down, their noseguard [Walter Tate] got it and then

Auburn scored on the field goal. Boy, I wish we hadn't tried that dadgum play.

One of Bowden's biggest flops came in a 30-26 loss to Southern Mississippi to open the 1989 season. It was something he borrowed from basketball, but a play that involved three quarterbacks was hardly a slam dunk in a game played at Jacksonville.

I got the idea for this play from watching Dean Smith's Four Corners offense in basketball. The idea was to freeze the ball. What I was trying to do was keep my quarterbacks happy because I couldn't play them all. We put in Brad Johnson, Charlie Ward, and Casey Weldon in at the same time. And P.T. [Willis] was our starter that year. And sometimes I believe he was in there with it, too. Every day after practice I would meet with the three quarterbacks and practice this little thing we called "four corners." Bill Peterson, when I was an assistant under him, would always do tricks at the end of practice. I picked it up from him and did it at West Virginia University and some here.

With this play, we did it for fun against our defense and thought that it just might win a ballgame sometime. I would put two of the quarterbacks wide, about 18 yards back so nobody could get to them real quick. One would throw the ball to the other quarterback, and that person would hold on to it. And when the other team would get close, he would throw it to this guy until somebody opened up downfield.

That last time we had the ball against Southern Mississippi, we put the three quarterbacks in there—Brad Johnson, Casey Weldon, and Charlie Ward. But they just laid everybody back there and let you do all of that. We didn't get any pressure. Where a play [usually lasts] five or seven seconds at the most, it seemed it ran like 20 seconds. What happened is when we tried this against Southern Mississippi, the clock ran out. Can you believe that? The dang clock ran out.

The game ended with this trick play failing as Weldon threw an incomplete pass to Ward.

Bowden is known for being ahead of the times when it comes to play calling and apparel. (Photo courtesy of Bobby Bowden)

Are You Missing Something?

Once, a Florida State opponent had help in its preparation for trick plays because of something left on the team plane—that something being the Seminoles' game plan. Bowden vaguely recalls the situation. Former assistant Jim Gladden fills in some of the details.

"We got on a plane to go play a game, and one of our players left his game plan, scouting report, and all of that in a folder," Gladden says. "When the plane dropped us off, they picked up Memphis State or somebody and flew them to their game. Those coaches got it and called the opponent and told them about it."

On another road trip to Auburn in 1983, Bowden's staff had gathered briefly in the team motel's hospitality room to watch a local station's Friday night news. Jaws dropped as they watched footage from one of Florida State's practices that showed a trick play the Seminoles had drawn up especially for Auburn. A Tallahassee television station had sent the Alabama TV station film from practice as part of a tradeoff, not realizing it had a play of interest to the Tigers' coaching staff.

Bowden explains that isn't unusual.

Hey, I've seen it happen to an opponent. You're watching TV highlights, and there in the background there is a trap that you didn't know they had. Then you go in there and start working on that thing—"We got to stop the trap."

That kind of thing happens a lot. You play somebody, and it seems like everything you do, somehow they knew. They probably don't. They just did a great job of scouting you. We've never been in one like where somebody wired your locker room. But you worry about that.

One of those games came against Clemson a year after Florida State pulled off the Puntrooskie.

"Danny Ford beat the pants off us," former assistant Wally Burnham says. "Everything we did defensively, they had an answer for. We thought they had snaked us. You always worried about somebody up on the bridge [that overlooked the practice fields]. You just kind of felt that they had a spy at practice."

It wasn't long after that, I think, that I closed practices for good.

Gene McDowell, who as an assistant coach under Bill Peterson was given orders to spy on a Penn State's practice for its 1967 matchup with Florida State, explains that clandestine activity was once part of the game.

"It was unusual for coaches to get access to that kind of information, but it wasn't unusual for them to attempt to get it," says McDowell, an inside linebackers coach under Bowden for 11 years. "I remember well before the rules were changed, coaches used to spy on practices.

"Now Bowden never did that—he never sent anybody to do clandestine research on the opponent. The subject never came up."

Bowden recalls plenty of times where Florida State received unsolicited tips. Sometimes, they worked against Bowden.

We've had a lot of times where we've been told—"They have a fake punt in. You watch out for that." It could be somebody who lives in that area.

I always remember when we played Pitt in that [1983] game where I drove off and tore up the bottom of my car. We were told all week that Dan Marino had a sprained ankle and could hardly walk. Before that game, he looked like 100 percent to me. He beat us that day as usual.

[Then-Pitt coach] Jackie [Sherrill] was bad about that kind of stuff. It was typical of a lot of Bear's boys. But it's strategy.

Like Sherrill and his Panthers, Jerry Claiborne didn't usually need help when he brought his Virginia Tech team to Tallahassee. But Bowden chuckles when he tells of the time when Florida State took hospitality to the extreme. Bowden was a Seminoles assistant at the time.

Jerry Claiborne came up after the game and said, "Here's your game plan. You left it in the locker room." I don't know how it got in that visitor's locker room, but it did.

"Don't Tell the Kids"

Bobby Bowden could hardly wait to unveil a special surprise he had for the Florida Gators in 1983. Florida State had not defeated its archrival in Gainesville since 1979. But Bowden remembers being hopeful that an offensive package his coaches introduced during the extra week of practice might do the trick in reversing fortune.

And why shouldn't he have been optimistic? Less then 10 years into his Florida State head coaching career, Bowden was building a reputation on the field as a successful gambler who parlayed trick plays into an edge over more talented, higher-ranked opponents.

Florida's defense featured All-American Wilber Marshall, whom Florida State and Florida had fought for in an intense recruiting battle. Yet Florida State coaches had confidence in the offense and the tricks they had planned for the Gators.

We were playing Florida, and we put in a certain formation with certain plays. We had worked on it all week. One of our players told his daddy—"Daddy, we're going to do this tomorrow, and you're going to see me do this. They don't know we're going to do it."

The way I understand what happened next is that his daddy goes to a party in Gainesville the night before the game, probably some alumni/booster meeting. And he goes and tells somebody, "My son is going to do this tomorrow—be watching for it."

And some Gator heard it and told the Florida coaches. Now we came out and tried it, and their defense moved right on it. They knew exactly what we were going to do.

Bowden allows he should have figured something was up during the game. Florida was ready for Florida State and forced a half-dozen turnovers en route to a 53-14 loss. But Bowden says it wasn't until a Florida coach kidded him about it years later that he discovered just how a formation that the Seminoles had worked so hard on had failed so miserably at Florida Field.

That's why to this day, a lot of times when I want to run a [trick] play in a game, I'll tell the coaches, "Don't tell the kids. Don't tell the kids."

I don't want them to know until we're in that game and get ready to do it.

The Butler Told It

That was a lesson Bowden says he learned not only against Florida but, as he notes, later in the most famous of his trick plays—the 1988 Puntrooskie at Clemson.

LeRoy Butler, the future Green Bay Packer, was central to making the fake punt work. He picked up the ball that was placed between Dayne Williams's legs and ran 78 yards to the Clemson one-yard line. Butler's dash set up a Florida State field goal and a 24-21 victory.

Butler, unbeknownst to Bowden until much later, almost caused the play to fail.

During the week before the game, Butler gushed about the play to his former Jacksonville Lee coach, Corky Rogers. And proud Coach Rogers told a gathering at his house the night before the Clemson game: "For those of you who are going to watch the Clemson game, LeRoy called me and said they are going to run a fake punt to him."

Former Clemson offensive lineman Wes Mann was at Rogers's party, and by phone, he reached a student manager at Clemson's team motel in Anderson, South Carolina. The student manager relayed it to the Clemson coaches.

"Yeah, I called [Rogers]," Butler says. "I told him I may have this chance at this great play. I don't think we'll run it. I never told him, 'Don't tell anybody.' I thought it was fun that he knew, and that they knew, and that it worked."

I didn't know about that until years later when it was written up. I'm sure glad I didn't know that [before the game]. If I had, I would have never run it. Isn't that funny? If I had known that, I wouldn't have run it.

One in a Million

Florida State opponents have benefited from other forms of eavesdropping during the Bowden era. Bowden now chuckles about the means by which Auburn, in 1985, nearly snuffed out one of his all-time favorite trick plays.

We had a fourth-and-one play that we knew would work. Because on fourth and one, they are coming at you. They ain't paying attention to nothing except stop that one-yard [run]. We worked all week on that play. The quarterback was going to fake the handoff, hide the ball, and then we'd send Hassan Jones down for a long one.

But we couldn't ever find a place to run it. I'd tell [offensive coordinator] Wayne McDuffie—"Dadgummit, we can't ever get them in a fourth-and-one where we can try this play."

So they were beating us pretty good [31-17]. It was late in the third quarter, and we were down on about our 40-yard line. We had a fourth-and-two, and they know to watch out for a trick. But I'm going, "Let's go. Let's do it."

Now we line up in that formation, and they do exactly like we want. Their safeties come flying up there.

The only potential snag came when Danny McManus left the game in the first quarter. McManus was still feeling the effects of a concussion he suffered two games earlier at Nebraska.

Backup Eric Thomas was behind center when Florida State ran the play. But just as Bowden planned it, Florida State faked a tailback dive and completed a long pass—about 48 yards—to Jones to set up Tony Smith's two-yard touchdown with less than five minutes remaining in the third quarter.

He created this play while watching practice earlier in the week, but it first came to him while watching film of Auburn safeties in short-yardage situations. Bowden introduced it to the offense just minutes after scribbling it in a notepad that is always in hand.

"He made our guys on defense close their eyes and cover their faces with their arms and some laid on the ground with their back to the offense, as Coach Bowden showed each offensive player where he wanted him to go on the play," former Florida State coach Wally Burnham laughs. "'Don't peek!' he'd shout."

Brad Scott, too, has trouble retelling the story without chuckling.

"He'd say, 'Hassan, you're going to come in there like you're going to crack on this linebacker—and you're not going to throw [a block] and miss, but you're going to dive on the ground,'" Scott recalls. "'Not roll one time but two times and get up and take right off and go to the goalpost. And tailback, you're going to cross your arms and dive over them. And quarterback, you got to have guts like a burglar and stick that ball in your stomach and just walk with your back turned to that line of scrimmage.' He'd get on one knee like a defensive end—'I see the ball. I see the ball. You didn't turn your back enough. Get the ball in your belly.' He'd get obsessed with it."

Bowden's attention to detail on trick plays comes down to this:

If they do good, everybody loves you. If a trick play goes bad, it can make you out to be the dumbest guy in the world. A trick play doesn't come with a guarantee. But you can help the odds by studying film. I used to get involved with teaching, no matter what the play, but not so much any more. A lot of times I will when I put a trick play in.

The other thing I do is test it against our defense [like the play against Auburn]. After I showed the offense how I wanted the play to work, I looked at the defense and said, "Try to stop this."

If our defense chews it up, then that probably means it is no good.

But what does it mean when the defense knows it is coming and the play still succeeds? Bowden says he didn't find out until years later during a trip to Auburn after the Florida State series had ended, and his son, Terry, was the head coach, that the Tigers coaching staff knew the Thomas-to-Jones play was coming.

I think that's what made it even more special. [Former Auburn defensive coordinator] Wayne Hall was telling me they heard me call the play. And they are trying to scream out on the field, "It's a fake, it's a fake!" Their kids couldn't hear them, and we successfully ran the trick play. Wayne and the other coaches said they knew about the play and still couldn't do anything about it.

How did the Auburn defensive staff know what Bowden was calling?

When the Tigers won big on October 12, 1985, the Tigers coaching staff boasted something else in addition to a running back named Bo Jackson. Auburn coaches had the frequency to the wireless microphone that Bowden wore as part of a pioneering all-access television documentary—the kind that became so popular 10 years later. The show was the brainstorm of WFSU television producer Gary Yordon, who would later become a Leon County commissioner.

Yordon and his crews shadowed Bowden and the Seminoles that entire season for a documentary titled *Finding a Way*.

Well, when Gary Yordon wanted to do this thing on me—he wanted me to be miked for all these games. And I asked him, "Is there any way anybody could intercept this?" He said, "There is no way anyone could ever pick this up. No way. It would be one in a million that they could pick up this channel we have it on."

Turned out, the odds were a lot less.

Fans in packed Jordan-Hare Stadium, trying to tune into the game, found a chatty Bowden instead.

What happened is somebody in the stands had picked it up on his radio. He goes upstairs into the box and tells the Auburn coaches—"I got his plays. I can hear every play Bobby Bowden is calling."

And then Auburn coaches got it—every play I called.

Wireless communication was a new technology, and Yordon found out later that the mostly concrete structure of Jordan-Hare Stadium conducted Bowden's microphone differently than in the steel erector set that was then Doak Campbell Stadium.

Actually, more than one Auburn fan had found Bowden on the FM dial, as Yordon later learned from his position in the press box. He had asked the person next to him to turn up and radio, so he could hear the play-by-play.

"All of a sudden I hear Bobby on the sidelines," Yordon says. "I had a walkie-talkie, and I tried to tell my crew to turn of the mike—'Turn off the...' They couldn't hear me. They're on the opposite side of the field, and it took me 25 minutes to get down to the field."

By the time Yordon had reached the sidelines, Auburn had the game firmly in control.

During the entire time Bowden was wearing the wireless microphone that season—on the field, in meetings, at the hotel, and in the locker room—Yordon says there were only six times Bowden cussed.

"The guy just doesn't cuss, but I got three of them after the game," Yordon says of his discussion with Bowden.

Yet Bowden didn't have a full grasp of how much damage that wireless microphone did until years later.

They beat us real bad that day. Real bad. Years later... Hall and the coaches were laughing and kidding me about it—"We got all your plays. We heard every play you were calling."

It's funny now.

But against an opponent that Bowden struggled to beat in the early years of his Florida State career and at a time when Seminoles fans were questioning his play calling, Bowden wasn't laughing.

I'd call a play and go, "Boy, what a dumb call. How did they know I was going to do that?" A guy intercepts the ball, and it's like he knew the play.

He did. And Florida State lost 59-27.

Too Cute

You have to be careful to not get too cute with them trick plays.

That's what happened against Nebraska in 1985 when Bowden attempted to run a shovel pass.

It was something a little different, and we didn't think the crew working the game had seen it before. So I explained it to them [before the game]. "Look, we might do this shovel pass. It's a pass, not a lateral, you see. So if something happens not quite right—we drop it—that's an incomplete pass and not a fumble."

I didn't do that with the Puntrooskie. We had worked on it, and I felt good about it, but I never even thought about it until the game got going. But a lot of times I'll say before the game, "Look, we might do this, and this is how it works. So you all don't blow the whistle dead on it." And we've had that happen before on a trick play where the ball was hid so well, they blew the whistle and killed it.

Yet despite all of Bowden's precautions, the officiating crew working that 1985 Nebraska game made the wrong call initially.

WFSU documentary producer Gary Yordon's cameras were rolling.

"We see him call the play, and sure enough, the football is dropped and two officials signal that it's Nebraska's ball," Yordon recalls. "The whole [Florida State] staff comes out shouting that it's an incomplete pass and not a fumble. And then you see the head referee coming up to Bowden saying, 'We got it, Coach. We got it, Coach. You told me about it.'"

But many of Bowden's trick plays work, and his son Terry says he knows why they often do for his dad and not for other coaches.

"I often thought of my dad on the sidelines when he was calling plays as a stand-up comic," Terry Bowden says. "A great play caller is a stand-up comic. He knows when to deliver the punch line. When to slow down and stretch you out and when to lead you on or down the wrong path for the punch line. People either get it or don't. You got to have timing.

"There's probably a generation that doesn't know this—but he's probably one of the greatest play callers there was—as far as taking plays and manipulating defense. It was like chess—setting up plays with plays.

"What fascinated me when I was on the staff was how much Dad would have a trick play he really wanted and it had to be a third and two or on the left hash. He would be wasting plays to get into a third and one on the left hash.

"'George, I got to have a third and one on the left hash.'

"'Well, Coach, I think we can score.'

"'No, no, get me a third-and-one on the left hash because when I get third and left hash, I know what they are going to be in and I know I got a trick play that is going to work.'

"If it was second and five, it would be, 'Don't give me a first down.'

"Dad's early football was not about being wild but being unpredictable. The whole philosophy of his offense was not having 50 plays but what you do with the plays you have. His basic background, like he always taught me, is never put in a play unless you can take one out, because you can't add time to your practice schedule. You got to keep your plays to a number you can execute.

"Let's say all you got is seven plays, but the defense knows at any time you could run one of those seven plays: That's unpredictability. 'The Riverboat Gambler' is just a matter of being unpredictable, and he did have those great special plays that nobody else did."

NFL scout Jim Goodman saw that timing work for Florida State from the opposing sideline as an assistant coach at Florida and later Clemson.

*Bowden's trick plays have usually been fan favorites at Florida State.
(Photo by Phil Coale/Sunset Images)*

"He was the master of that," Goodman says. "He just had uncanny timing. And if you ever pulled a trick play against him, that was something. We faked a field goal against him in 1992 when I was at Clemson, and it went for a first down. I was so proud. We did a trick play against him."

Bowden would rather be measured not by trick plays but by his team's execution of all plays and whether it was fundamentally sound. But he understands what he'll be remembered for most on the field.

If you play better fundamentals than your opponent, you could neutralize their talent. I'd rather for them to say he's an excellent coach than a trick coach. But I don't mind the trick thing.

The legacy I would want is that he did it the right way. I'd hate to leave a legacy that put Florida State on probation for cheating [and] that I ran over people. I would want my legacy to be that I did it the right way.

Chapter 3

Recruiting

Part I
Building a Powerhouse

In the Dogs' House

Ron Simmons made his way into Florida State football lore by posting a 525-pound effort in the bench press and then becoming Bobby Bowden's first consensus All-American. Along the way, he made five sacks and 19 tackles against North Texas State in Tallahassee as a freshman and finished ninth in the Heisman Trophy balloting as a junior in 1979.

But Simmons first made Bowden's day on the recruiting trail. In 1977, the defensive lineman from Warner Robins, Georgia, selected Florida State over Georgia.

"Simmons was the first real marquee guy we were able to land here at Florida State," longtime Florida State assistant coach Jim Gladden says. "When I first came here, we were picking up leftovers after Auburn, Florida, Georgia, and even Miami had first picks."

Bowden will remember the recruitment of Simmons for the twists that happened along the way.

Ron Simmons was probably the best recruiting story of my time. You just don't go into Georgia and easily get a player. He had exactly what you were looking for. And he showed it right away.

My first year, '76, we had one of the worst defenses in the country. We were scoring points, but we couldn't stop anybody. Next year we had eight of them coming back and put Ron Simmons at nose guard. One guy made a difference. First game we played when he was a freshman, we beat Southern Miss. He blocked a punt for a touchdown as a freshman, and we knew we had something good here.

I'll never forget this about recruiting him. He had already committed to Florida State. A week before signing day, Ron Simmons is at his high school basketball game, and [former Florida State linebackers coach] Gene McDowell is up there watching him. Now I'm down here in my office, and Gene calls me and said, "Coach, you got to get back up here. Ron Simmons says he's not coming to Florida State. He's mad as heck. He's as mad as can be."

I asked what happened.

And Gene said, "They announced on television tonight you are going to Ole Miss as the head coach."

Georgia got the guy at the television station to say that. That's how far Georgia went on this. He announced that Bobby Bowden is in line and is expected to get the Mississippi job.

Well, Ron thought I had been lying to him all this time. I had to get in my car and drive up there.

And then we couldn't find him. We thought Georgia must have hid him. And Gene finally found him. We sat him down and said, "Son, someone is just lying about that."

He was OK after that. That was a real trick they played on us.

I thought it was [Georgia], and the guy who [leaked the false report] at Georgia—he isn't there now—told me about it later. He said, "You didn't know we did this to you, did you?"

And I said, "I thought you did."

McDowell found Simmons a day later with longtime family friend Bill "Stump" Franklin, who just happened to be a former player of Bowden's at South Georgia College. The businessman owned Franklin's Battery and Electric store in Warner Robins.

"In those day, hiding players—that was not illegal. That was pretty routine stuff," McDowell says of the practice of keeping prospects from competing schools in the final days or hours before signing day.

"We didn't know it, but it was our guy that hid him. 'Stump' was able to convince him there was nothing to the story."

Bobby Pope was the sportscaster who broke the story of Bowden's departure to Ole Miss. At the time, Coach Ken Cooper was under pressure in Oxford, Mississippi, following two consecutive 6-5 seasons.

"Sam Mitchell was a coach at Georgia at the time, and he gave me word that Coach Bowden was going to Ole Miss," says Pope, now the athletic director at Mercer University in Macon. "[He said,] 'The word is out, and you ought to use it on your sports show.' And I did.

"Coach Bowden called me up and told me it wasn't true. And the next morning I did an interview in Warner Robins with Coach Bowden—that he was staying at Florida State."

"That was really the key ingredient in getting Ron Simmons," McDowell says. "Bill Franklin had kind of adopted Simmons when he was a child. He had him working around his [battery store] since grade school, so whatever 'Stump' told Simmons to do he was going to do it. And that was the reason we got him. 'Stump' really respected Coach Bowden."

Under the NCAA's less stringent rules of the times, Franklin was Bowden's contact, and the Franklin house was Bowden's "motel" on recruiting trips to Warner Robins.

"Stump" had told me about him and said, "I think you can get him down there." We recruited three guys off that team. Ron Simmons was the No. 1 prospect in Georgia. James Brooks went to Auburn, and James Womack went to Georgia.

Back in those days you could go up there and stay as long as you want to. I'd go and stay the night with "Stump." "Stump" and his wife had two young kids. They shared a room on my visits, and I stayed in somebody's bedroom. I can remember getting up at two or three in the morning, and having an idea about how to convince Ron [to sign with Florida State].

I went and knocked on his bedroom door and said, "'Stump,' I know what we can do. I know what we might do [to get Simmons]."

It was a battle right up until Ron signed his name.

"They're With Me"

To recruit LeRoy Butler in 1986, Bowden and recruiting coordinator Brad Scott went into the bowels of one of Jacksonville's most crime-riddled areas. A Duval County deputy who had befriended Scott on his frequent visits to Jacksonville was so disturbed that Scott had gone into the area alone, he invited him along on a night shift into Butler's neighborhood. The reality check worked.

"Right away we saw a guy stabbed within blocks of LeRoy's place," Scott says.

Scott's future visits to Butler, who became a Florida State All-America cornerback and All-Pro safety with the Green Bay Packers, were more cautious. For Bowden, dangerous neighborhoods came with the territory. And still do.

One place, there was gunfire outside while I was talking to a prospect and his mother.

Me and Chuck Amato went to recruit Henri Crockett, and he had told Chuck—"As you go down so-and-so street, there will be a lot of guys out front. Don't stop. Don't stop." We drove down three more blocks, and he was standing outside his house making sure we got there.

When we recruited LeRoy, Brad had told me that LeRoy didn't want us going in there alone. So he worked it out that we would meet him. I'm not sure there's been something like that since. There were all these people around—LeRoy was special to his community, and I guess this was kind of a big deal.

Scott says "big deal" falls short of describing the scene.

"LeRoy tells me, 'Coach, do not come in here [with Coach Bowden] without calling me and let me meet you two blocks away,'" Scott says. "That area was heavy with drugs and crime.

"Everybody would wave when you came in with LeRoy. He was a folk hero to that community. He was hope.

"The day Coach Bowden came in there, LeRoy meets us, and I mean people were on the sides of the street like it was a July Fourth parade as you got closer to his house.

"You'd hear people shouting, 'There's that Bobby Bowden.'

"And LeRoy would yell back, 'They're with me.'"

"A Deal Sealer"

By the winter of 1991, Mickey Andrews and his defensive staff had become adept at spotting lightning-quick athletes who matched Florida State's evolving aggressive defense. Deion Sanders's basketball moves six years earlier had convinced Andrews that he had found a big playmaker despite his lack of All-America or even All-State credentials because of a knee injury. Marvin Jones, one of six *Parade* All-Americans signed in 1990, ran the 40-yard dash in 4.5 seconds and needed half that time to dismantle opposing running backs.

It was Bowden's job to close the deal, and he usually did that with banter about common acquaintances or experiences.

"That's the way it is with Coach; it don't take people long to be like family with him," Andrews says. "The interesting thing is he enjoys meeting people. He really enjoys getting into the home. It's amazing."

In addition to establishing himself as "The Riverboat Gambler" and as the coach who turned around the Florida State football program, Bobby Bowden became known as a top recruiter. His folksy way with mommas helped him sign 23 future consensus NCAA All-Americans and become Division I-A's all-time winningest coach.

"He didn't talk Xs and Os," former linebackers coach Wally Burnham says. "Somebody would mention a name, and he'd say, 'Do you know so-and-so?' And whether Coach Bowden knew him or not, he would make people think that he did. He got next to those mommas and daddies."

Scott, who served as Bowden's recruiting coordinator in the late 1980s, says it didn't take much preparation for Bowden to take over an official visit.

"He would know [about] the kids beforehand. But I'd give him this cheat sheet—'The momma loves to do this, Dad does this. And this certain thing will be on the TV set, and this is why it's important to them.' He'd study that [sheet] and take over, and you'd just sit over there and smile. And they would be, 'My gosh, it's like he's known us for years.'"

And you would always have photos that he'd sign, put his little love note to the mommas.

A lot of times I put "Love you," and mommas love that.

Florida State assistants quickly learned to get out of the way when Bowden entered a residence for an official visit.

"When you take Coach Bowden in, you don't do the talking," Gladden says. "You may break the ice and start the conversation, but when you bring him in there, it's his show. You let Coach Bowden lay down his deal. Some guys didn't understand that, and in the staff meeting on Monday, he would be, 'Buddy, if you are going to do all the talking, there isn't no need for me to go.'

"The way he said it would be so funny, and everybody would just crack up."

Ann Bowden calls her husband a private man.

"He likes to come home, get into his shorts, and watch TV or [game film]," she says. "We don't do a lot of socializing."

But Bowden shines in public, and his coaches say Bowden is especially animated on home visits during recruiting.

I accept the fact it's part of the job, and I prepare myself mentally to enjoy it. I have to talk myself into it.

I would rather be alone. It's like at night; I would rather go home. People ask me if I go to a basketball game or baseball game. And I say if I get a night off, which isn't very often, I go home.

Ann has always got on me about this because Ann does enjoy that—being out there, socializing with people.

Going back to when Ann and I first started dating—Ann likes double dating, and I always prefer just going out as me and Ann. And I'm still that way. I like to go out with Ann, and occasionally Ann and I and another couple. Occasionally.

I am a private person. But once I get into it, I do enjoy people and enjoy finding out about people. And that's the way I am recruiting.

Very seldom do I talk Xs and Os. I will, if a coach tips me off that this kid wants to know about how you are going to use him in the system or things like that. But most of the time they've already covered that. I'm going in there to meet the parents and try to sell them that they want to play for the program and me.

The main thing I try to be is to be honest. I never have promised a kid he will start. I might say, "I hope you can start, because we need immediate help at your position." That's the way it was with [offensive lineman] Jamie Dukes. I told him, "If you don't start, it will be your fault." And he started every game in his career [and earned consensus All-America honors].

I try not to say anything negative about an opponent. Now a lot of people misconstrue that—when it comes to comparing my school to that school, I may try to show why mine is the best. If I'm stronger in this area, I try to bring it out. I wouldn't go in there and say, "You see what happened over yonder— you don't want your kid involved in that."

Family was what Bowden was prepared to talk about when he met Derrick Brooks's family in 1991.

Brooks possessed speed, size, and smarts, and Notre Dame, Miami, and Florida were among the schools pursuing Brooks. *USA Today's* Defensive Player of the Year in 1990 finished with a 3.94 grade point average. Not every high school

Bobby Bowden and Derrick Brooks celebrate the 1993 national championship. (Photo by Phil Coale/Sunset Images)

All-American pans out. But from the first handshake, Bowden figured Brooks was the real deal.

> *Some players you just have that sense about. I knew he had all the intangibles. He was a great student and had great desire to succeed. That was very evident in high school. We also knew he would be a great player if we put him in the right place. We thought he would be a safety because it was very evident he liked to come up. He didn't like to go back. The first year he played safety, and then we moved him to linebacker. He got bigger and could fly and was a great leader.*

Bowden was right. Brooks, an anchor on Florida State's defense during its 1993 national championship run, became a two-time consensus All-American, the recipient of an NCAA postgraduate scholarship, and an All-Pro linebacker for the Tampa Bay Buccaneers and in 2003 was appointed to the Florida State Board of Trustees, the school's governing board.

Bowden arrived in Pensacola ready to make the pitch of a lifetime.

"We went into Derrick's grandmother's house," Mickey Andrews remembers. "We go in, and Coach is talking on one end of the sofa. Derrick and his folks are all there, and we're talking.

"The little girl came over there and laid her head down in Coach's lap. Before you knew it, she was sound asleep just like a family member had come over."

The little girl was Brooks's sister—Latoya—who was about four or five at the time. Bowden still pokes fun at himself over it.

I put her to sleep. Boy.

Hardly.

"When she did that—I was coming to Florida State," Brooks says. "That was the deal sealer when she fell asleep in his lap."

Sight Unseen

Bobby Bowden knew exactly what to expect from the last scrimmage of the 1989 preseason camp. Or thought he did.

We took our best against the rest. All the good players are over here, and all the other guys are over yonder, and this team [of the good players] is supposed to run up and down the field. And the game is going to end up 50-nothin'.

But Charlie Ward nearly beats the first team. Game probably ended up 33-28. We could not stop him—he was just making up stuff.

That's when you really realized we got something here, boy. It was just amazing. It made you feel like maybe we're not very good,

Bowden and Charlie Ward strategize on the sideline during the 1992 Miami game. (Photo by Phil Coale/Sunset Images)

but then you realize we got this one individual you couldn't stop— running and throwing the football.

I thought he was going to be more of a running quarterback because that had been his style in high school. He could throw better than I realized.

This was affirmation of what Wayne McDuffie had spotted on the football fields and basketball courts of Thomasville, Georgia, in 1987. It was why McDuffie and receivers coach John Eason so passionately pushed for Ward in a conference room full of doubters—Florida State assistant coaches—during the late stages of the 1987-1988 recruiting season. Ward may have been Georgia's top offensive player, but most Florida State assistants weren't convinced. And although Bowden wasn't sure whether a mobile Ward would fit into Florida State's offensive scheme, he didn't stand in McDuffie's way.

> *Wayne McDuffie insisted we take him. I didn't get to see Charlie before we signed him. Florida State had not had a black quarterback before Charlie. I had two black quarterbacks at West Virginia, and there was probably criticism back in those days [at West Virginia] from some fans.*
>
> *There is one thing about coaches—they are not prejudiced. They are going to play the best guy they can play. Wayne drove me up to Thomasville, and you couldn't help but be impressed with his family. He had just wonderful parents. He had exactly what you were looking for in him.*
>
> *We sign him. When he came in here, boy, were we happy.*

Of course, Ward became a Heisman Trophy winner in 1993 and led Florida State to its first national championship before enjoying a long career as a professional basketball player.

He is also symbolic of Bowden's willingness to take a calculated risk off the field and on the recruiting trail. Bowden turned around the Florida State program and built a dynasty with more than 60 *Parade* All-Americans during his first 29 recruiting seasons. But an equally important ingredient in Florida State's success was the large group of lesser-known prospects who were offered scholarships or encouraged to walk on with Bowden's strong endorsement.

"You would find a guy you would really like, and maybe nobody wanted him," Gladden says. "There were a bunch of guys like that. Keith Jones, Monk Bonasorte, Danny McManus, Charlie Ward.

"Keith Jones [now a color analyst for the Sunshine Network]—nobody wanted him. I'd come in with film on this guy, and say, 'Coach, I got this kid. He's salutatorian. He can run, and he's the quarterback. This guy is an outstanding person, and he's going to make this university proud.'

"And he would say, 'Let me see some film on him, babe.'

Bowden stood behind Casey Weldon during his recruitment, and Weldon returned the favor with a stellar career. (Photo by Phil Coale/Sunset Images)

"He looked at the film five minutes and said, 'You go tell them guys I'm backing you. I'm signing him.' [George] Haffner didn't want him. Jack Stanton didn't want him.

"[Jones] started four years here.

"Coach Bowden had a good eye for seeing talent that would fit."

Brad Scott credits Bowden for backing him when the case was being made for Casey Weldon, who went from Tallahassee's North Florida Christian to Heisman Trophy runner-up in 1991.

"I saw him in a playoff game," Scott says. "He had such poise and presence back there, and everybody was worrying about his arm strength. He cut loose a couple of big throws in that game. I came back excited about him. Coach said, 'If you feel so strongly about him, we need to offer him [a letter of intent].' And he turned out to be a pretty good player for us.

"After that, and I don't know if it was because of that, Coach Bowden just trusted his recruiting coordinator. My recollection is he would let me make the final decision. But he did want to see quarterbacks."

Current recruiting coordinator John Lilly said Bowden's feel for potential goes beyond the initial recruiting process. He is one of many assistant coaches who say Bowden is excellent at evaluating talent.

"[Former tight end] Ryan Sprague is one Coach put on scholarship early in his career," Lilly says. "You respect what Coach is doing, but when he put Ryan on scholarship, I didn't think the guy was going to ever play. But he ends up starting most of two years.

"Coach Bowden can detect certain things. Just seems to be something he's a natural at."

That Dunn Boy

Warrick Dunn's game-winning touchdown against Florida in 1993—a play so memorable to both Bowden and Florida State fans—began with a fake handoff from Charlie Ward and finished with Dunn dashing 79 yards into the Florida end zone after a pass from a scrambling Ward.

It was a designed play. But it was not part of the design Florida State coaches had for Dunn when they recruited him out of Baton Rouge, Louisiana, earlier that year.

The interesting thing about Warrick Dunn is how we had him penciled in as a defensive back. We already got [Rock] Preston out of Miami, and we were only looking for one running back. We

Warrick Dunn (28) dashes away from the Gators to score the winning touchdown in 1993. Bowden figured that Dunn would be a defensive back and not a tailback when he was recruiting Dunn out of Baton Rouge, Louisiana. (Photo by Phil Coale/Sunset Images)

didn't have any more offensive scholarships to give. Mickey had one left and said, "We'll offer it to that Dunn boy."

We told him, "We are offering you a scholarship, but it is a defensive back scholarship. Are you willing to play defensive back?"

"Yes, I'd be willing to play defensive back," was his reply. "That will be all right, but would you give me a chance to play tailback?"

"Yeah, I'll give you a shot at it. But I just want you to know, if we need you at corner, that's where we'll play you."

So he comes in, and we had three tailbacks returning. So it looks like he's going to play corner. Then Tiger McMillon got hurt [in preseason camp], and you had Sean Jackson and Marquette Smith. That's not enough tailbacks, so now we had to move one of the freshmen up. Rock Preston is the guy we would have brought up because he is from [the state of] Florida. But he sprained his ankle, and we had to bring Dunn up. He got in a couple of scrimmages, and it was obvious this guy needs the ball under his arm.

Nearly every recruiting season, Bowden's staff must juggle the personnel needs of the team with the wants of the prospect.

Bowden's son Terry says he can point to at least one time when he was certain he caught his dad promising a prospect one spot and planning for him to play another.

"Dad and I were recruiting Laveranues Coles out of Jacksonville," Terry Bowden says. "He wanted to be a running back.

"I said, 'Son, Florida State is going to make you a receiver.'

"He said, 'No, they won't. They promised.'

"And I said, 'I know too much of their situation. I know their receivers coach [Terry's brother, Jeff]. I know their head coach. They are not going to let you be a tailback. I know the scoop.' ... They had somehow slipped it out the summer [before] that they were going to recruit him as a receiver.

"I tell him that at Auburn he would be a great tailback. But he signs with Florida State. And, of course, when they sign him, they immediately move him to receiver."

Well, not immediately. Coles approached Bobby Bowden about more playing time before the Miami game, the fifth of the 1996 season and Coles's first game at Florida State. Bowden countered with a proposal to move Coles to wide receiver, where he started one game that season and saw significant playing time as a first-year freshman.

If I give them my word, that is it. I can't lose that. Or then they will mistrust you, and trust has got to be there.

We've had a number of guys come here promised a position, and then maybe they see a better opportunity elsewhere. If I promise a kid he will be tailback, he's going to be tailback. Now Greg Jones would have been a heck of a fullback, but we promised him he would be tailback.

Anquan Boldin was a great high school quarterback, and he wanted to be a quarterback at Florida State. I said, "I want you as a quarterback." And if I tell you that, I won't ever move you unless you come and say, "Coach, I want to move."

It was firm. And I'm sure one of the reasons he picked Florida State is because I guaranteed him he could play quarterback. And he would have played quarterback all four years if he wanted to. But he wasn't here two days [in 1999], and he came in this office, and said, "I want to be a receiver."

I said, "Are you sure about that? Have you talked to your daddy about that?" His daddy is a graduate of Georgia Tech and is pretty sharp. He said that's where he should have been. He could play immediately at wide receiver.

Lorne Sam—he wanted to be quarterback. I said, "No, we want you as a wide receiver. If I ever do that, if I say you got to be a wide receiver, you got to be that."

By the Letter

The framed letter has been hanging in the Weinkes' basement trophy room since the winter of 1991.

Jan. 21, 1991
Dear Chris,
Thanks so much for your Christmas card. Coming from you it really means a lot to me. I think of you often and your family and the great visit we had a year ago at this time.

I sure hated to lose you to baseball, but if that is what you wanted, that is what I wanted. Chris, I do want you to keep one thing in mind. If baseball does not work out for you, I hope you will come on back here and play football. I have had a lot of quarterbacks in my 38 years of coaching but I have never had anyone that I thought would be a better prospect than you. I really think you have all the tools. With about 3 1/2 years of college football you could be a No. 1 draft choice. Probably be worth many millions and millions of dollars. Now knowing you and your quality, you might do the same thing in baseball, but if it ever does not seem what you want, I hope you will get in touch with me immediately and we'll get things worked out. Now I'm not trying to talk you out of your commitment. You have got to do your best in reaching your present goal. I am just saying that if your elbow, shoulder or something knocks you out of baseball, I still think you can be a great football player and we would love you to have you here.

Give my love to all the family and I will always consider you one of mine. Thanks again for your note and have a wonderful 1991. I will be keeping up with you.

Sincerely,
Coach Bowden

Bowden hasn't seen it since sending it to Weinke after the *Parade* All-American from St. Paul, Minnesota, packed up and left the Florida State campus just days into his collegiate football career in 1990. A $600,000 bonus from the Toronto Blue Jays was too much for Weinke to walk away from, and Bowden—tantalized by Weinke's ability—couldn't say anything to make him stay.

"I thought my mind was made up when I came down here—that I would stay," Weinke says.

When Weinke changed his mind after four days in Tallahassee but before he had enrolled in school, Bowden made a promise to his family that the door was open for him to come back. After six years in the Blue Jays organization without making the majors, Weinke was ready to try Florida State. Again.

When he went to baseball, I wrote him that letter but never expected to hear from him again. I remember Mark coming up to me and saying, "Guess who I heard from? Chris Weinke wants to come back."

I responded, "What do you think? Is he too old? Does he still
have his legs? Can he still play football?"
   I remember Mark saying, "If we take him back, we're going
to lose this guy [the other recruit] whose football is all ahead of him.
Chris might be over the hill."

The other guy was Drew Henson, who was on the brink
of committing to Florida State during his junior year of high
school. Henson would later do a flip-flop of Weinke's career
path and sign with the New York Yankees before returning to
football with the Dallas Cowboys.

   The second time with Chris, we were recruiting Drew
Henson, who went to Michigan. He was willing to commit to us as
a junior if we wouldn't take any more quarterbacks. Just like Chris
Rix committed to us as a junior and stuck with it.
   We were about to set that up; Mark was working on getting
that commitment even though it meant we wouldn't sign another
quarterback.
   So then about that time Chris [Weinke] contacts Mark Richt
and asks him, "Would you still take me back? I think I'm through
with baseball. Would you all be interested in me coming back here?"
   We talked about it, and we both agreed that we promised we
would take Chris back. We did and lost Henson. It was a great deci-
sion we made somehow.
   The thing that Chris gave you was a guy who could think like
a coach instead of a young guy who might do anything. I always felt
like playing baseball really helped his poise. I don't know how you
can stand in that batter's box with somebody throwing a 90-mph
fastball at you and you not have a lot of poise.
   Now after he threw those six interceptions I began to wonder
if he lost it. We beat Texas A&M in that first game [in 1998], and
then he threw those six interceptions [against North Carolina
State], and you wondered. But that was brief. You quickly knew he
was the guy.

Weinke had to display that poise during his bid to return to Florida State. Although Bowden stood firmly behind his promise to Weinke, he allowed Richt to play hardball.

"Drew Henson had come to our camp going into 10th or 11th grade, and we were very impressed with him," Richt says. "I met his father, and they were getting ready to come to Tallahassee. I believe they were going to commit to Coach Bowden and seal the deal a year in advance. Then about that time, Weinke pops up.

"I was very concerned because I thought Henson was going to be a very good player. I knew once Weinke got in the picture we were going to lose Henson. Just the presence of Weinke [at Florida State] wouldn't have been as attractive a situation for Drew.

"I asked Coach Bowden for permission to talk to Weinke straight up. I didn't want Chris to come in and a semester later and say this was for the birds, and in the meantime, we lose Henson.

"Weinke was in town, and we went into the QB meeting room. Coach had made the promise to him years ago, and we were never going to say, 'You couldn't have this scholarship.' That was never a consideration.

"But I wanted to see if he was serious. I talked to him about Dan Kendra and the chances of beating out Kendra may not be good. I was just about trying to talk him out of it just to see how serious he was.

"I remember Weinke said, 'Coach, I understand about competition. I just have one question—if I'm better than Kendra, will I play?'

"I said, 'Yes, you would play.'

"He said, 'Then OK, I'm coming.'"

Weinke enrolled at Florida State in January 1997. He was 24. The quarterback led Florida State to its second national championship. And during that perfect season in 1999, Weinke became Florida State's second Heisman Trophy winner.

Bowden also won over another fan.

"When Coach Bowden told me that I could come back, I believed him," Weinke says. "There was never a question for me. Regardless of the situation. The thing I expressed to them was that, 'I don't know if I can still play.'

"His reply was—'I made a promise to you, and you're more than welcome to come back. We're not guaranteeing anything, but we'd love to have you back.' I don't know if that would be the case at a lot of other places.

"I bring the letter, I bring that story up as just kind of an example when people ask me what Coach Bowden is like. He told me something seven years earlier and kept his word.

"People say you don't pick a school because of the coach, but in a lot of ways, I did."

Part II
Reality Checks, Relatives, and Religion

"I Know Who You Are"

As Florida State's primary recruiting coach in Dade County, Kevin Steele didn't give much thought to his passenger's notoriety as he made his way through the Miami traffic. Steele, hired by Florida State in 2003 to be its linebackers coach, had worked for Tom Osborne and Johnny Majors. Bobby Bowden was just another legendary coach whom Steele could call boss.

"I had been with head coaches before where people would take a second look and say, 'Aren't you so and so?'" Steele says. "But with Coach Bowden, it's like you're with the President.

"This one trip in Miami, there was a wreck and construction, and everything was down to one lane; we couldn't move. It's lunch hour, and we're just sitting there in the car, and this one guy is shouting, 'There's Bobby Bowden.' And before you know it there is this crowd of people up at the windows and staring into the car. And Coach Bowden is waving.

"About 20 minutes later we get to the high school. There's a bunch of city workers across the street at this park clipping hedges and mowing. And one of them recognized Coach Bowden, and they come over in a wave. One goes back to the truck and gets this pocket camera. And they take pictures with him. And when they go back across the street, they are high-fiving each other because they just met Bobby Bowden."

Nearly every assistant who has traveled with Coach Bowden has a story about Bowden's popularity. Mickey Andrews tells of the time they were recruiting together in Alabama and a prospect's mother asked him to stop by a beauty salon to say hello to an uncle. Within a minute of pulling in front of the shop, people climbed into the vehicle just to say hello to Coach Bowden. The player signed elsewhere.

I tell the coaches to try to stay away from this thing—there are some people who want me to come down there knowing they aren't going to Florida State, but they want Coach Bowden there. They want to see Coach Bowden.

This has happened several times where I go down there, and there are seven cars outside. You go in there thinking, "This is going to be pretty good—they got all these people pulling for us." So you go in there, and you sit, talk, and laugh and sign autographs and get your picture taken with everybody.

You leave, and you got a pretty good feeling. The next morning you read in the paper he just committed to Florida. You've just been had. He knew where he was going before I ever walked in the door.

I've gone into a home and talked to the family and the mom is reading a magazine, and you walk out knowing you're not getting that kid.

Recruiting coordinator John Lilly says that even after seven years of being on the road with Bowden, he sometimes finds himself in awe of the reception Bowden receives at high schools or at sporting events.

"But really anywhere you go with Coach Bowden, it's that way," Lilly says. "It's neat driving around with Coach Bowden. He is who he is. He's not caught up in any of that.

"I'll never forget when we were down in Pahokee [recruiting Anquan Boldin]. You'll sometimes have time from when you get to a place to when you are supposed to visit or attend a game or whatever you are there for. We had some time, and we went to Burger King to eat, and there were probably three people in there and two were working. Within three minutes, there were 30 people in that Burger King because somebody got on the phone and said, 'Bobby Bowden is here.'

"They were getting him to sign napkins and whatever they had."

Bowden says he takes it all in stride. He's had enough lessons "in comeuppance" on the recruiting trail throughout the years to know to check any ego before takeoff.

One such time came when assistant Jim Gladden and Bowden were traveling together in the Jacksonville-South Georgia area. The Florida State season had ended with a victory over Florida, and the two took a break from bowl preparation to recruit.

"We pull into an oil station—kind of one of these gun-barrel stores—one of them long ones with an old creaking screen door with a sign that says, 'Batter whipped bread,'" Gladden says. "There's an old potbelly stove in the back there and a guy sitting there with bib overalls. He gets up, and I'm thinking he's recognized Coach Bowden. He's coming up to him to talk to him.

"'I know you, I know you,' he says."

Bowden takes over the story from there.

Well, I'm out there getting the car gassed up. And you hear him, "I know you, I know you."

So I'm thinking to myself, "He's going to say that you're the head coach at Florida State. And maybe congratulate you on the way things are going." I'm feeling pretty good about what's about to happen.

When he comes up to me, he says, "I know you. I know who you are. You are the guy who sells them Fords on TV."

He put me down real quick.

Beaten by the Bear

Long before Bowden won himself a few football games at Florida State and promoted trucks and burgers on television, he received his first dose of recruiting reality. And it came from his childhood idol—Alabama legend Paul "Bear" Bryant, whom Bowden passed in career victories in 2003. Bowden was a Florida State assistant coach under Bill Peterson when he had a recruiting encounter with the "Bear" in the mid-1960s.

I can remember going up to Ozark, Alabama, trying to recruit a quarterback named Joe Kelley. I was an assistant coach here. Joe was an excellent thrower, and he liked us because we were throwing all the time, and 'Bama was probably running the wishbone at the time.

So I go visit him. I had a great visit, and he was interested in us. He was a passer, and 'Bama was going to run the ball. I'd tell him, "Don't go up there; they ain't going to throw it." Alabama was like Georgia; it was hard to get somebody good out of that state. But I felt we had a chance. And I was feeling good about the visit.

I hear a car pull up outside, and then I hear somebody walking up the steps and shuffling their feet.

So I finish my business, and Coach Bryant walks in when I walk out. I'm still thinking I had a real good meeting, and then I get back and get the word he committed to Alabama.

Bowden (bottom row, far right), as an assistant coach at Florida State, cut his teeth on the recruiting trail against his childhood idol, Bear Bryant. (Photo courtesy of Bobby Bowden)

Somebody probably called Coach Bryant and told him, "Coach Bowden is up here from Florida State. You better get here." That happens a lot. Probably he flew down there.

He walked right in there and put that Bear Bryant magic on him, and there the prospect went.

That wasn't the first rejection I got at Florida State. Also, when I was an assistant, I was recruiting a fullback from Milton.

Spent a lot of time with him. So I go over there—it's getting close to signing day. He has a real sweet mother, and she cooks me a delicious meal. He's a fine young man. So we're at the table, and we're having a nice meal, and I got around to it—"Have you decided where you are going yet?"

And he said, "Yes."

And I ask, "Where?"

And he said, "Auburn."

That's the sweetest turndown I ever had in my life.

The first rejection I got here after I became [head coach] was in my second year recruiting here, 1977. [Former Florida State running backs coach] Nick Kish was recruiting a kid out of Sarasota. Good-looking tackle. Nick had worked on him so hard. Nick takes me down there a week before signing day to get the kid to commit to me. And Nick is telling me, "He's going to tell you he's coming to Florida State." I'm all set for that, happy and every-thing—Nick's got him. Nick's got him.

So I ask the kid if he knows where he's going yet. And, of course, I know he's going to commit to us. So I ask him.

And he says, "I'm going to Florida."

Poor Nick, it killed him—just broke his heart. Most of them, when they aren't going with you, they'll call you. They don't usually do it in person.

That's tough, especially if you have to go far. I remember when we were recruiting [quarterback] Jared Jones out of Walla Walla, Washington. Mark [Richt] wanted me to go out and look at him. I said, "You're wasting my time. He's not coming way down here to go to school." But Mark said, "We can't get him unless you visit, and if you do visit him, I think we'll get him." And we did, but at the time I told him, "You better be sure, because he can tell me no over the phone."

It is the preferred way to be rejected by a prospect. A phone call saves money and time. Bowden's disdain for just hanging around doing nothing while on the recruiting trail or on the Seminoles Boosters trail is legendary among the Florida State athletic staff. He despises making trips for naught.

"He's a guy who he'll do anything if he feels you can get the guy," Gladden says. "But if it's a wild goose chase—

"There was one time John had him out to California on Super Bowl Sunday and he said, 'Isn't that Super Bowl Sunday, buddy? We better get him [if I'm going to miss the game].'"

Brad Scott points to the recruiting of former Florida State linebacker Kirk Carruthers, whose father was a former coach under then-Michigan State coach George Perles. The younger

Carruthers lived in the shadow of the Spartans' stadium when Florida State was recruiting him.

"I pop in a tape of him, and you can see he is very athletic," Scott says. "But Bobby is, 'Wait a minute'—he can see Michigan State's stadium from his door. [He said,] 'I'm not interested in just flying up there. It's cold up there in Michigan.' And Coach doesn't like cold. He wants it 300 degrees in the car when you are traveling with him. And the other thing about Coach Bowden is he wants to sleep in his bed. His thing always was, 'I'll fly anywhere in the world, but I want to be back in my bed before the next morning.'

"We get him to go up there to visit Kirk and his mom. There is ice on the runway and snow just about everywhere. Coach does his usual great job with the son and his mother, and we get him."

Wally Burnham is proof that taking Bowden on a wild goose chase isn't a "fireable" offense. But on a long trip from Fort Myers to Tallahassee in 1987, he wondered.

"I was recruiting [lineman] Peter Rausch, and Peter was about to make a decision," Burnham said. "I got Coach to go down there and visit him on a Saturday. The plan was to get down to Fort Myers at 8:00 a.m., have breakfast with Peter and his mom, and get back to Tallahassee in time for everything to get started for the recruiting weekend.

"We fly down there on the state plane. We get there, and I knock on the door, and all of a sudden I see this little piece of paper taped to the door. On this piece of paper it says, 'Coach, sorry we could not be here. We had to go shopping.' And it was signed by his mother.

"We get stood up. I thought I was going to be fired. That's the most scared I've ever been.

"He didn't say a word the whole way back. And he never mentioned it again. That's the way he is. If you do something, he moves on past it. I could have lost my job over it, I'm sure."

As the note foretold and Washburn feared, Rausch's interest had wavered; he later signed with Notre Dame, and Bowden's trip was for naught.

Burnham was on another trip that didn't go as planned. But this time—on an official visit to *Parade* All-America linebacker Ken Alexander in 1990—Bowden didn't mind.

"It's down to us and Notre Dame," Burnham says. "So we get there, and we sit down, and I can hear him talking in another room. And he is talking to Peter Cordelli, a coach at Notre Dame. So I'm thinking, 'Here we go.'"

Bowden shared the same thought.

Any time back in those days you were recruiting against Notre Dame, you aren't likely to get them.

"He sits down, and Coach Bowden unbuttons his jacket and started his speech," Burnham continues. "Ken had heard enough speeches from coaches by that time to know what was getting ready to happen.

"So he said, 'Wait a minute, Coach. I'm committing to you right now.' And he stood up and walked over to Coach and shook his hand.

"Well, he caught Coach so much by surprise. He had flown all the way to Austin, Texas, and didn't get to deliver his speech.

"He got that look he can get and finally said, 'Well, you just ruined my speech.'

"Everybody laughed."

Your Momma Called

Bobby Bowden has bumped into Bear Bryant, Joe Paterno, and Tom Osborne among other legendary coaches as he has made his rounds on the recruiting trail during his Florida State days as an assistant and head coach. Bowden says the encounters were always cordial.

But he could always count on some friendly fire, when he rubbed shoulders with two particular coaches—sons Terry and Tommy.

Tommy still gets some good ones in on me. He'd tell them how I used to beat them—like I'm a bad guy. I used to run into Terry a lot recruiting—especially down in Fort Lauderdale. Auburn had its foot in the door down there in a couple of high schools. He beat us on a real good defensive back down there one time.

Terry told the mother [of one prospect] I wouldn't be coaching but for a couple of more years. "Don't go to Florida State, Daddy won't be coaching. He's already 63 or something."

I go into the home, and they tell me what my son had said— "That you won't be coaching but a couple of years." They kind of laughed. I said, "I tell you what, I'll be coaching at Florida State longer than he'll be coaching at Auburn."

That's a statement I wish I hadn't made.

Bowden's comments came prior to the 1993 season, Terry's first at Auburn. Brother Tommy was his offensive coordinator.

"We were recruiting Lewis Battle from a little ol' town above Auburn," Terry Bowden said. "He was a big-time recruit—a defensive back/wide receiver. We were kind of mad at Dad because he's having great years. And here he has to come to Alabama—45 minutes from Auburn—and tries to come in here and steal a player from right under our noses, which is going to make us look bad.

"Dad and I talked about a lot of things, including recruiting, and now in my first year he's going to come in and get players just because he can. It made me mad—'Dad, you snake.'

"Tommy and I go to this player's house the last week before signing day, and we just tear Dad apart. 'He's 63 years old, and you'll be lucky to have him around when you go looking for a job and you want the coach to recommend you. You better know every golf course in Florida, because that's where he

Bowden and son Terry (left) still get a good laugh over their recruiting encounters. (Photo by Phil Coale/Sunset Images)

is going to be—on a golf course, retired. And when he comes to visit you—speak up, because he's hard of hearing.'

"Everything we could think of, we said. Lewis's high school coach was there, and my dad was coming in the next night. That coach told my dad everything we said. Everything. That's when my dad grabbed the kid and said, 'I heard all the stuff my son said, but I promise you one thing—I'll be at Florida State longer than he'll be at Auburn.'"

Terry Bowden left Auburn during the 1998 season and now as an ABC Sports college analyst offers commentary on his father, still coaching at Florida State.

Another story the Bowdens love to tell on each other took place in 1995 in Fort Lauderdale, where both programs were interested in highly regarded safety Martavious Houston out of Boyd Anderson High School.

That's the one I got on Terry about his momma.

Terry Bowden picked the last Thursday before National Signing Day to see Houston at his home.

"I figure I'll lock it up with a six o'clock visit," Terry Bowden says. "I figure other coaches have home weekend visits and wouldn't be able to see him on Friday, and I'd get the last visit.

"It's down between us and Florida State. I really loaded him up with all that we have going for us at Auburn. He wouldn't commit, but I knew I had him locked up. As I get to the porch to say goodbye, my dad has pulled up and walked up the front sidewalk.

"My dad had planned the visit right after me. Dad gets up to the front porch, and in front of Martavious and his mom, my dad pats me on the top of my head and says, 'Terry, when you get home, your momma wants you to call.'

"That's all he said. I'm thinking, 'You rat.'

"What do you think this player and his mom thought? 'Your momma wants you to call.'

"When I tell people this story, my comeback is, 'And I never once mentioned his drinking problem.' Of course, I didn't do that in front of the kid. That was the last head-to-head between us."

Tommy and his father continue to see each other on the recruiting trail. They still exchange banter, and Tommy, Clemson's head coach, pokes fun at his father in front of prospects.

"It's an icebreaker going in the home," Tommy Bowden says. "I'll say, Daddy is coming in here, you better go hide your silverware. He used to beat us, and all that.

"The retirement, I don't use that. I don't even touch his retirement."

"Preacher Man"

Brad Scott learned early in his role as Florida State's recruiting coordinator, just as Bobby Bowden did against the "Bear," that there is no such thing as a sure thing. And that was especially true in Central Florida, where the Florida Gators had dominated recruiting for years.

But Scott had reason to feel good, when he and Bowden walked into running back Reno Fells's Palatka home in 1985. Fells's mother was a minister, and Bowden speaks at churches throughout the country on the Sundays of his off season. Scott figured she and Bowden, a lay minister, had plenty in common, and he left the two to talk in the kitchen.

I'm in there talking religion with her. I knew she was a very religious woman—a minister—so I was talking religion with her. I told her, "I'm a member of the Baptist church."

I tell her that, and she came back and said, "I used to be Baptist. But we've been saved, and now we're Christians." That was the funniest thing.

So I guess it didn't bother her too much.

I will not force religion on them. If I see a Bible on the table, I might go from that. When we begin the year each fall, we take our boys to church. I'll usually bring that up [during official visits] and let them know their son doesn't have to go.

All I'm trying to do is show them they are welcomed in this town by all the churches. I know how it is when kids go away from home for the first time—I was the same way. The first thing you do is resign from the church. I turned in my resignation. "I'm not going any more."

I just want to show them churches, and then it's up to them.

Part III
Road Trips with Bowden

Two Pilots and Two Props

Flying is so much a part of our business. Especially recruiting. So you just have to do it.

I won't get in a plane unless they have two pilots and two props. I am not getting on any more planes unless they have two engines. If one of them goes out, you still have a chance.

Two pilots I had used a lot died in crashes.

And I can tell you two planes I nearly was on I could have died. I nearly took the head coaching job at Marshall [after the 1969 season]. I was an assistant at West Virginia, and they offered me the job, and I really contemplated taking it. But I felt like I could get a bigger job. The next year, the team plane crashed into a side of a mountain and killed everybody on the plane.

And then I turned down the LSU job [in 1979], and Bo Rein, who had been at North Carolina State, got the job. He was killed the next spring recruiting. Something went wrong with the plane, and they both went unconscious and flew out over the Atlantic Ocean. That could have been me.

I don't recall any [automobile] accidents.

But he has his been in situations that made him uncomfortable on the road and put the assistant coach who was driving in Bowden's doghouse. One of those occasions came during the 2004 recruiting season when John Lilly was driving Bowden and assistant coach Jimmy Heggins to meet eventual signee Kenny O'Neal at his Oakland, California, residence.

"It was dark. I was coming up on the exit I needed on the freeway," Lilly said. "Right before we got there, I saw another sign, and it confused me … And then I realize I'm going to miss my exit, and it's not going to be easy to get back where I need to be, and we don't want to be late.

"There's this concrete barrier, and I go beyond it. I look back and see that I have plenty of room to back up. It gets kind of quiet, and Coach Bowden is saying, 'You know, statistics show a high percentage of accidents are caused by people backing up on the freeway.'

"I knew he wasn't real happy about what I was doing, but I figured that was better than the alternative of going on and trying to get back and maybe getting lost.

"It gets real quiet, and finally there is an opening, and I'm on the exit we want. After we get going again, finally Coach Bowden breaks the silence by saying, 'I guess you don't care about the statistics, do you, buddy?'"

Bowden doesn't smile when he recalls Lilly's dangerous maneuver.

Dadgum John. As much as I've read about highway safety— one on the worst things you can do is miss an exit and try to back up. That's one of the big ones. And John did that.

Golly, it scared me to death.

Now here's a funny one. It's Martin Luther King Day, and I'm with [former assistant head coach] Chuck Amato, and we're in Miami [in the Liberty City area]. Chuck had been recruiting in Miami a long time and really knew his way around that city.

But, wouldn't you know it, Chuck takes a wrong turn. We get down a wrong street, and [there is] a parade.

This is the stuff of legend in Miami, and certainly among Florida State coaches. Bowden in the middle of a Martin Luther King Jr. Day parade waving to everyone. There's only one problem with the image.

"We are one block down from the Martin Luther King Jr. Day parade. Not in it," Amato said. "We get to 'Snoop' Minnis's house, and I told Coach Bowden, 'I'll tell you what—we were a block away from the parade, but by the time Friday comes, you will have been in that parade the way stories grow. It didn't take that long. We were going around Wednesday recruiting, and people are saying, 'Coach Bowden, I heard you were on a float in the parade.'"

Laughs on the Road

A trickster on the field, Bobby Bowden appreciates a good prank pulled off it. His favorite on the recruiting trail came at the expense of Jim Gladden. In 1985, Sammie Smith had surpassed Ron Simmons as the most sought-after and highly decorated prospect.

When we were recruiting Sammie Smith, he's probably the hottest prospect in the country—225 pounds with world-class speed. Everybody wanted him.

We go down there to [Zellwood] and visit him, and all the time Jim is telling me, "He's coming. He's coming. He's going to tell you tonight he is coming." So we go to his house, and we're all sitting there, and Jim said, "Well, Sam, have you made up your mind where you are going?"

And Sam said, "Yes, sir."

"Well, tell Coach Bowden where you are going."

"I'm going to go to Michigan."

Jim liked to faint.

Smith recalls that he sold the trick too effectively. He upset his mother in the process.

"I had just visited Michigan, and it really came down to Michigan and Florida State," Smith said. "Coach Gladden knew there was a chance I might go to Michigan, so I just threw it out there at him to play with him.

Sammie Smith went from coveted prospect to a talented tailback for Florida State, but not before he played a joke on Bowden and assistant coach Jim Gladden. (Photo by Phil Coale/Sunset Images)

"I didn't let anybody know I was going to do that. I didn't even tell my parents. And when I told Coach Bowden I was going to Michigan, my mother was so upset, because my parents loved Florida State and this is where they wanted me to come."

Thanks, Coach

Free time with Bowden on the road is usually filled with naps or eating. Bowden, of course, is notorious for his catnaps, which can be taken at any time and any place. An insatiable appetite for reading—especially military books—and catnaps are Bowden's ways to fight stress. He keeps one book in his office bathroom, one in a bathroom at his house, and always one in his briefcase.

If I have a lot of worries—I hate to say worries because you aren't supposed to worry—I'll say concerns, then I go [read] a book about World War II and bring back old memories and think of my childhood. I look at photos from a trip Ann and I took. A nap helps.

This job has stress. I can really feel it when that last game is played. And then you go through recruiting, and you go through it again. You lose a kid, it's like you lose a game. It's like two times when it's like, "Oh boy, I'm free." One is the last game of the season, and the other is when recruiting is over.

Now I'd rather do this [coaching] than anything else. But I have my ways of handling the stress, and the most important is having your priorities in the right place. Faith, family. Don't let football be life or death.

"We were over in Jacksonville recruiting and leaving LeRoy Butler's house going to Edgar Bennett's," former recruiting and offensive coordinator Brad Scott says. "And he asked, 'How far do we have to go?'

"I said, 'Coach, five to 10 minutes.'

"And he'd go, "OK, wake me up when we get there.' I'm talking as soon as he said that, he'd be asleep. Almost snoring. How he does it, I do not know. He'd wake up refreshed and ready to go."

Mickey Andrews cracks up just thinking about the noisy drive down the freeways of Los Angeles on a recruiting trip two years ago.

"We got a bunch of coaches in there, and everybody is talking on their cell phones setting up the next stop," Andrews says. "There's all this buzz, and Coach is sound asleep."

Coaches and the Florida State support staff digress from the subject of recruiting when they recant their favorite story about a Bowden catnap. Florida State had lost four in a row to

Miami when the Hurricanes came to Tallahassee in 1989. Miami was ranked second, and the craziness surrounding the game had spilled into Bowden's office. He decided to seek refuge in the locker room, where he found a metal chair, leaned up against the dry eraser board, and promptly went to sleep.

"I'm looking at my watch. I don't see Coach, and it's almost time for him to start his speech to the guys," sports information director Rob Wilson says. "He starts it about six minutes before the game, and it usually lasts two minutes.

"I look for him, and he's in the chair leaning up against the dry eraser board right in front of where the whole team had gathered for his speech. I run up to Chuck Amato and said, 'You got to wake him.' And [he says,] 'I'm not waking him up.' So I get real close to Coach and yell, 'Five and a half minutes until kickoff.' He shakes a little, jumps up, and his speech was basically, 'Let's go out there and get them.'

"Before, everybody was kind of nervous. I think that helped the players more than anything, seeing how relaxed Coach was."

Florida State won, 24-10.

Back to recruiting, catnaps were not the only source of laughter for Bowden's assistants. Gladden and Bowden were together in Tyler, Texas, in 1997 on a recruiting trip to see David Warren, *USA Today*'s Defensive Player of the Year. The two had already been to Warren's high school and had some time before they would make a home visit.

"So Coach asks me, 'Jim, you hungry? Let's find us a hamburger stand.'

"He sees a Burger King and tells me to pull up in there. So we go in, and he says to me, 'Eat what you want, buddy. I'm paying.'

"So I go up there to the counter and get a big meal. And he pulls his wallet out and starts giving them coupons. That's when he was doing those Burger King commercials and he had all these coupons.

"So he was, 'I'm paying,' and then he uses those coupons."

Another humorous moment came on the road when Bowden was traveling with Wally Burnham.

I was down in Auburndale—that's where Terrance Barber, who played for Florida, is from. I think I was speaking at his banquet that night. We had some time, and I decided I needed a haircut. I bend down and split my britches. I mean big.

What Wally Burnham won't forget is the trip to a nearby mall to get another pair.

"He had split his pants all the way down," Burnham said. "He just tied his coat around his waist and walked in the mall like that was just a normal thing."

Chapter *4*

Bowden Behind the Scenes

Part I
Bowden and His Coaches

Coach, He's in the Bathroom

Of the six offensive coordinators who have worked under Bobby Bowden at Florida State, Bowden says none was more hard-headed and intense than Wayne McDuffie.

Bowden says McDuffie, his offensive coordinator from 1983 through 1989, was "a tough nut, but I loved him."

I called up there to the coaches' box looking for Wayne McDuffie—"Wayne, Wayne."

And the reply from one of the other coaches would be—"Coach, he's in the bathroom."

The game would still be going on, and I'd call a little later, and the reply again would be, "Wayne is in the bathroom."

I found out about it after the game that Wayne got mad at me because of some play I called. And he just left. They would say he was in the bathroom, but he would just leave.

I called him in the next day, and we had a little talk. We won the game and we were ahead at the time he left, or I might have handled it differently.

I probably didn't know a lot of this. We were so far ahead is when he left a lot of times. The first time he left—somebody told me. And I told him not to do it again.

One time, according to current videographer Craig Campanozzi, McDuffie was involved in an automobile accident a few blocks away from where the Florida State game was still being played.

Florida State assistant coaches Jim Gladden (left), Chuck Amato, and Mickey Andrews yell instructions and check on their players on the field. (Photo by Phil Coale/Sunset Images)

"Wayne wanted more control of the total offense, and Coach Bowden didn't want to relinquish that," former assistant coach Jim Gladden says. "And he thought trick plays were hot-doggy. Wayne McDuffie left the box a bunch of times. McDuffie would leave the coaches' box in the third quarter and go down [to the locker room] and watch it on TV."

Brad Scott, then a tight ends coach, found himself sitting next to an empty seat that minutes before had belonged to McDuffie. That was the first time he had to cover for the offensive coordinator.

"Wayne had some nerve. When Wayne would leave, it would be one of two things," Scott explains. "He'd be mad or frustrated that the play he had suggested [down to the field] didn't get called, or there was a great game on that night that had already started and he wanted to go the locker room and watch it.

"We were fully in control in the game, and Wayne left. And there's Coach Bowden calling for Wayne. The only thing I

The view from the coaches' box has not always been what the assistant coaches for Bowden want to see—especially when Bowden calls a reverse. (Photo by Phil Coale/Sunset Images)

could think to say was that he was in the bathroom. That was kind of the standard answer.

"He's trying to find Wayne, and this time Wayne is mad and left the game because Wayne called for the sweep and Coach Bowden called the sprint draw ... and Wayne would take it personal.

"I'd come to work early on Monday, and that's when Coach Bowden would have his sessions with Coach McDuffie. It would start at 6:30. I'd never hear Coach Bowden raise his voice except in those meetings. Wayne would walk out mad and red with his veins sticking out and Coach would act like nothing happened. It didn't affect him. That's the way Coach Bowden was—he could move on."

McDuffie was the most demonstrative of any of Bowden's offensive coordinators when it came to objecting to Bowden's play calling. Bowden says that was especially true behind closed doors.

Not so much at the time [of the decision] but back in the office he'd come in and gripe like mad. He and I had some blowouts in my office and behind closed doors.

Every once in a while I will slip in [a cuss word], but I try not to. I try not to use it on purpose. One of my real bad habits coming up in life is to get real mad and swear.

Wayne was stubborn, and I liked him because of that. He was one of the toughest guys I worked with and the most controversial. I don't like "yes" men. "Yes" men bother me more than anything else 'cause you might want to do some strategy that is wrong, and if they agree with you just because you are the boss, you get yourself beat.

Life would be easier if you didn't have [confrontation], but if you are going to be in my position or [a sportswriter's] position and there are no confrontations, you are getting nothing done.

Defensive coordinator Mickey Andrews remembers an exchange between McDuffie and Bowden during the 1985 Auburn game in which Bowden was trying to set up the play in which Eric Thomas faked a tailback dive and threw long to Hassan Jones.

Bowden repeatedly urged McDuffie to get into a fourth-and-one situation so he could execute the trick play against Auburn.

"And ol' McDuffie answered back, 'We don't have a dadgum call to get it in fourth and one,'" recalls Andrews.

"You're Fired"

Terry Bowden was a Florida State volunteer coach assigned to help offensive coordinator George Henshaw in the early 1980s. The third oldest of Bowden's sons missed McDuffie's stint as offensive coordinator, which followed Henshaw's. But that doesn't mean he isn't above giving his dad grief for McDuffie going AWOL during a game.

"That's a classic," Terry says. "That's one for the book—your offensive coordinator walks out and leaves the stadium.

"When I was at Florida State, Dad was still calling plays at that point. George Henshaw had moved from defensive line coach to offensive coordinator. Being on the defensive side, he had studied offenses, and he knew the offense better than you would think.

"I remember a game, it was first and three on the three, and George Henshaw wanted to throw to the end zone. Dad wanted to do something else and told George, 'If it doesn't work, you're fired.'

"That was the first time I was around him when he fired his offensive coordinator, which didn't count once the game was over. He did that a lot."

His assistants may have bristled at such action. But Bowden, whose quick wit is well documented, insists the intent was often to lighten the situation.

Usually, I was kidding.

Bowden's firing of Henshaw during games became legendary among the Florida State's future staffs.

"I heard the stories where he fired George Henshaw 16 times in a year," Brad Scott says. "And one time at Miami, when Coach Bowden fired him on the spot, Henshaw threw all his papers into the air [from his coaches' box seat]."

Henshaw had followed Bobby Bowden from West Virginia to Florida State and was told he would get the first coordinator's job that became available. Because defensive coordinator Jack Stanton had a reputation of moving around, Henshaw figured that would be the position he would take over. But when George Haffner left after the 1978 season, Henshaw assumed the offensive coordinator duties. And the on-the-field firings commenced.

"I can remember Coach calling me into the office," Henshaw says, "and saying, 'George, just remember, whatever happens during a game doesn't count. If I fire you, it doesn't count.'

"It wasn't bad to disagree with him. I learned a lot in those days. He would call something, and you would think, 'This has got to be craziest call.' And I would say 90 percent of the time the play would work like a charm. It was like [opposing defensive coordinators] were playing checkers and he was playing chess."

Despite Henshaw's lack of offensive experience, he possessed qualities that Bowden says he still looks for in his offensive coordinator.

In an offensive coordinator, I want somebody who knows how to organize practice and has a good sound philosophy and doesn't get offended if I tell them do this instead of that. I'd rather them be fundamentally sound and basic and let me add the creativeness. I'd hate to bring in a creative guy who wasn't fundamentally sound. I wouldn't bring that kind of guy here.

I always thought a good coach is a good coach. Like a teacher is a good teacher. He might have to teach history, but then he might have to go over and teach economics. So I was fine with George becoming my offensive coordinator.

All of my offensive coordinators except Haffner have come from within my system. I've only had two defensive coordinators, and I brought both of them in.

Bowden admits to having fired three assistant coaches for keeps in his first 28 years at Florida State. Not one was an offensive coordinator.

I can remember three [assistants] whom I did fire— I felt like they needed to go.

I just don't like announcing that. I've never been one to do that kind of thing publicly. I don't like calling my players out in front of other players or to do that with my coaches.

I hate to have that put in the paper—"Bobby fired so and so."

I would say, "Look, it's best for you to leave."

One coach I had here—I hated to fire him. I said, "You are not going to coach next year. Now if you stay, we have to keep paying you, but you ain't going to coach." So he went and got another job.

It was rumored that getting a divorce was a fireable offense during Bowden's early years at Florida State. And Bowden, who celebrated his 55th wedding anniversary in 2004, says he did not knowingly hire a coach who was divorced at that time.

One prospective coach was going through a divorce when he was hired by Bowden in the early 1980s and then took steps to keep that fact hidden from Bowden. But Bowden recalls the coach's wife coming down for the interview and then not being seen again.

But years ago, Bobby Bowden changed his stance and hired coaches, including his son Jeff, who have been divorced. He changed his hiring practices regarding divorce before he brought in Jeff.

When I first started coaching here, I felt like we needed a coach to set an example for these kids. And that was one of the ways. Try to stay with it if you can. Divorce soon got bigger and bigger, and our society has gotten to a point where you couldn't hire any coaches. What, 50 percent of our families [in the nation] are divorced?

"You Got to Be Tough"

Mark Richt doesn't remember being "fired" while calling plays during his tenure as Florida State's offensive coordinator from 1994 through 2000. Florida State won a national championship during that time, and Richt coached Florida State's two Heisman Trophy-winning quarterbacks—Charlie Ward and Chris Weinke. Richt was also a rarity among Florida State coaches under Bowden. He and Daryl Dickey are the only coaches to leave for jobs at other schools and return. Both were volunteer coaches at the time of their first departure.

Bowden says that he doesn't hold it against a coach who leaves. When Brad Scott left for the head coaching job at South Carolina and took Wally Burnham and receivers coach John Eason with him, Scott's and Bowden's staffs immediately became embroiled in a dispute over the recruitment of Ben Washington. The Tallahasseean eventually selected South Carolina.

I don't hold that against them. Gosh, no. That's just football. When they left here, we had a back named Washington. Wally had been recruiting him, and I had wished Wally wouldn't recruit him when he went up [to South Carolina]. They kept recruiting and got him, and that upset me. But those things don't make me dislike them. It just shows me how competitive they are.

I might bring them back as long as they left in good standing. I don't like them leaving for a parallel job, but it's hard to talk them out of taking a good head coaching job.

As a volunteer coach and then quarterbacks coach, Richt had witnessed firsthand the relationship between Bowden and previous offensive coordinators Wayne McDuffie and then Brad Scott.

"I never felt he fired me," Richt says. "I don't think he ever used that word.

"The thing that he did, the more heated things got, he would be calling my name. And if he got more excited, he started calling Brad's name.

"And when he really got excited, he started calling for Wayne.

"I remember that happening every once in a while. He would get hot. If things weren't going good, it just wasn't a whole lot of fun.

"'Are you OK? Do you got a plan?'

"I would answer, 'I got it, Coach.'"

"It wasn't just awful, but he wanted to score and he wanted to score every time. It was a lot of fun if we were moving the ball."

The communication could be strained but lacked the edginess that sometimes appeared between McDuffie and Bowden.

"I remember one time, it was at the end of the game, and this [defensive coordinator] kept blitzing and blitzing," Richt says. "We were in some heated discussions as to what to do on certain plays. And they were pounding us with that blitz, and I think I called one play, and we ended up beating the blitz and scored a touchdown.

"And I say [over the headsets], 'There, you son of a you-know-what.'

"And you hear Coach Bowden say, 'You talking to me?'

"And I was actually saying it to the [defensive] coordinator, like, 'Quit blitzing, you big jerk.' And here Coach is asking me, 'Are you talking to me?' And I'm like, 'No, Coach, I was directing it to their defensive coordinator.'"

Beginning with Brad Scott's later years as the Florida State offensive coordinator, Bowden says he tried to be less hands-on while the offense was on the field.

I've been calling plays all my life. It's hard not to. I've done much better. You get to a point where a head coach can't keep up with everything. You just don't have time. I don't have time to study film as much as they can, because I got to go to this or I got to go to that. I eventually began to turn it over more to Mark, because I felt real good about him. But I got to interjecting a lot, and it really wasn't fair to him. I felt bad.

He came into to talk to me about it, and said, "Coach, it's driving me crazy. You keep interrupting me—Why do you do this, why you do that?"

I said, "Mark, I know it. I know it's not good. I wish I could stop. Mark, you are just going to have to be tough to put up with it."

I finally got where I didn't do it as much. As time has gone by, I don't do that as much, thank goodness.

Richt says it didn't matter much to him who called the plays, and he would make that point clear to his boss after a particularly difficult Saturday.

"I would humbly walk in his office and go, 'I don't particularly care who calls the plays, but I just want to make sure we are running a smooth operation,'" Richt says.

"I asked him a couple of times, not being a jerk but humbly saying, 'If you would like to take it over again, then I'm all for that so we can run smoothly. But if I'm going to be calling the plays, I'm having a hard time keeping my train of thought when you are constantly wanting to make a suggestion here in the middle of a drive. If we can have our conversations between the series, that would help.'

"Then he would be, 'You just got to tell me to hush and be tough with me.'

"I would say, 'You're my boss and I respect you, and I'm certainly not going to tell you to hush up in the middle of a game.'

"It would happen maybe twice a year—these conversations. And he would say, 'I'll stay out of it, buddy.'

"And he would stay out of it a game or two or a quarter or two. It was never controversial or a hot and nasty conversation. I would just plead my case, and he would be, 'Oh, I'm sorry. I need to stay out of it.'

"I don't want to make it look like I thought he was a pain in the rear, because he wasn't. He had good suggestions, but it was just different than my train of thought. For me to be effective, I couldn't constantly have other ideas coming in my head."

Jeff Bowden has had a lifetime as a Bowden to appreciate the situation he was inheriting from Mark Richt. His father promoted him from receivers coach to offensive coordinator after the 2000 season. With the introduction of the spread offense in the early 1990s and then the growth of Richt as offensive coordinator in the late 1990s, Bobby Bowden wasn't as hands-on as he was during the McDuffie and Henshaw years.

But Bowden allows he still has his moments of taking over, and Jeff says, when that happens, it doesn't matter whether you are the coach's son or Mark Richt.

"I don't think it's any different," Jeff Bowden says. "It is an understood role here for an offensive coordinator that [Bobby Bowden] is offensive minded. The one thing I appreciate is his not wanting to hold back. If you practice a trick play and don't use it—his famous line is, 'What are we saving it for?'

"As far as his input, that has to be assumed. I don't see a lot of difference [between his involvement with me and that with Richt].

"I can specifically remember going in and talking to him, because there was a lot of input when Mark was here, and I remember how hard it was on Mark to concentrate and have a train of thought. I went in [to Bowden's office] myself and mentioned to him that it was tough for Mark, because he gets it not just from Dad but suggestions from other coaches.

"Not [like] one conversation woke him up. But it made him a little more aware of how difficult it was. It would probably be tougher for somebody else when Dad decides to step in. I've grown up around it and just understand it."

"You Better Be Right"

I don't think I've been as bad since Mark [Richt], and I think I eased off Mark. I still will ask, "Are you sure this is what you want to do? Are you sure?" Sometimes I do that to test them. Because if they answer, "I'm not sure it will work," then I know I better get something else in there.

There are times now that I say, "Run this play," and [Jeff] better do it.

Mark is such a sensitive person. I'm sure I really caused him some bad nights. With Mark, I felt bad about it, but it's like they say, "The head coach might be wrong, but he is the head coach."

Bobby Bowden still studies film for hours and expresses his opinions and desires in staff meetings as well as Friday night's all important "iffy meetings," in which offensive strategy is reviewed in detail.

And he is the boss.

Brad Scott learned that lesson as a tight ends coach in 1985. And Bowden made the point with dramatic flair. Florida State was ahead of Nebraska 17-13 in the waning moments of a meeting between top 20 opponents in Lincoln, Nebraska.

"We had the game won," Scott recalls. "I was on the sideline and was kind of in charge of the two-minute offense in regards to where does it get to a point you can just take a knee and end it.

"It's down to the last possession [after Nebraska's last drive fizzled at the Florida State 42-yard line]," Scott continues. "I read all of Homer Smith's notes—he had a 50-page book on clock management. I had a little chart—one timeout means to do this, two timeouts mean this. We hit that magic point, but Coach is still wanting to run plays—toss sweeps—things with too much risk.

"And I'm saying to him, 'Heck, we got the game won, Coach. Take a knee. We don't have to run another play.'

"Things happen really, really fast on them sidelines. And he said, 'Are you sure on this? Are you sure?'

"I said, 'Yes, Coach, I've got the card right here. We got it won; all we got to do is take a knee.'"

Billy Smith (the Florida Highway patrolman in charge of Bowden's security) was standing right beside him, and Coach Bowden looked at him. Bowden still remembers what he told his young assistant.

"Brad, if you are wrong, I'm going to take that gun of Bill's and shoot you."

The thing I remember is you got the game won if you don't have to turn the ball over. If they don't get the ball back, you won it. There are guys around me who started celebrating, and I'm saying, "We haven't won this thing yet." What you'd love to do is [have] the quarterback take the ball and get on the ground and let 25 seconds go down. But if you do it too soon, uh-oh, uh-oh. There's still three seconds left.

It was one of the situations where I couldn't tell if we could kill the clock or do we need to knock out another first down.

And Brad finally said, "Coach, we got it if we take a knee."

And I asked him, "Are you sure?"

"Yeah, yeah, just take a knee the next two plays. We got it."

And that's when I told Brad—"You better be sure or I'm going to take this gun and shoot you."

Scott picks the story back up from there.

"Billy Smith's eyes got big. And I moved away from Coach Bowden, and I get on the phone to Wayne [McDuffie in the coaches' box] and say, 'Hey, McDuffie, I'm right, ain't I?'"

Scott was right, and Florida State had another important victory over Tom Osborne's Cornhuskers.

"The game is over, and Coach turns around and hugs me," Scott recalls. "And then he said, 'That's the way to be on top of it.'"

That exchange on the Florida State sidelines stuck with Scott as he made his way from tight ends coach to being in charge of the offensive line to offensive coordinator.

Two of Scott's favorite Bowden sayings also came before he took over the offensive coordinator duties. Art Baker joined the Florida State staff in 1984 and had introduced Bowden to the freeze option. That offense wasn't working in a late-season game against South Carolina that Florida State eventually lost 38-26. The Seminoles trailed 38-7 in the third quarter when Bowden had seen enough.

Bowden almost always has Billy Smith (right) beside him on the sideline, as he was here in 1990 when Florida State played Joe Paterno's Penn State team in the Blockbuster Bowl. (Photo by Phil Coale/Sunset Images)

"He got on the phone, and he gets us two quick touchdowns," Scott recalls. "That's one of those times when he said to us, 'Dadgummit, you boys are making a simple game way too hard.'

"In the course of another game, he had been wanting to run a sprint draw. And we'd say, 'Coach, you can't do that—that's unsound.' And sure enough, he'd hand the ball off to Sammie [Smith], and Sammie would make that guy miss and one other guy miss and break it for a long one.

"And Coach would get on the phone and say, 'You all think you're so smart. You young bucks talk yourself out of more good plays.'"

Bowden says the arrival of the spread and fast-break offenses made it more difficult for him to call plays from the sidelines. And gradually the bulk of play calling was handed over to Brad Scott and then Mark Richt.

"As we developed the spread stuff, Coach Bowden was less hands-on than during Wayne's time," Scott says. "He didn't like the motion offense. You start moving, showing motion, and he wasn't used to that and didn't know how to call it.

"One thing about it, though, you better by-golly be successful or your fanny was back in that I [formation]. You go out there and have two or three bad series, the headphones are coming back on.

"He'd slowly give it to you, maybe let you [take over the offense] in the first quarter, or for some games he just would say, 'You just plan on calling this one.' He wasn't real quick to get on the phones and take it away from you. But he would do that if it wasn't working after several series. He was not a coach who would immediately grab the headphones and say, 'You boys don't know what you are doing, and I'm calling plays.'"

Bowden says, when he does put on the headsets, it doesn't necessarily mean he is giving orders or presenting ideas. But Bowden finds it more difficult to call plays from his vantage point.

If we would sit out in the I formation, I could probably call plays again. If I'm sitting upstairs, I could call it. But with it spread out—well, the best example I've ever been able to give in explaining that is trying to play checkers at eyeball level [with the board]. You can't see the moves. I THINK there is one over there.

I don't usually find out what happens until Monday.

He laughs.

During a game, I usually watch their defense—seeing if there is anything I can pass on to the offensive coordinator.

If I put the headphones on it's probably to tell [the assistants] something I see and [to ask,] "Did you see it?" Or it may be, "Did you think about this or did you think about that? Have you tried

this or why don't you try this? Watch this corner over here, he's com-
ing up close." Or the worst thing I can say, which I just used to drive
Mark [Richt] crazy with, is, "Why did you do that?"

And it might be when I put the headphones on that we've
gone one and a half quarters, and we ain't done nothing. And I
might say, "What the heck is going on up there?"

Bowden directs most of his attention to the offense,
but defensive coordinator Mickey Andrews isn't immune to
Bowden's suggestions or verbal jabs.

I don't get very involved with the defense. Not very much at
all. When I first started out coaching—my first 10 years—I
coached it all. Until I came to Florida State in 1963 as an assistant
coach, I was a defensive coach up until then. My teams are going to
play defense and kick. That's the way I was raised. That's Bob
Neyland, Bear Bryant back in the '40s and '50s, and it's me. We
ain't going to win unless we play great defense. You might win eight
or nine, but you aren't going to win it all without defense.

It's like with what is happening with our basketball team.
Leonard Hamilton is a good basketball coach because he teaches
defense.

So defense is very important to me. But if I'm on the head-
phones with them, it's too much talking. I might suggest something
to one of the coaches or maybe Mickey. "Make the kids quit jump-
ing off sides," but not much. Occasionally I may jump in there. If
I can anticipate something the [offense might do]—"They look like
they are going to run that tight end drag."

One instance that still draws a laugh from Andrews came
against Auburn in 1984 in Tallahassee.

"It was in that game that Coach Bowden told us, 'Y'all
can't stop them; let them score in a hurry so we'll have more
time on offense.'

"On another occasion during that time, he had been after
and been after us to put in a 'sell the farm defense.' A sell-the-

farm defense is when you blitz everybody. You don't have a free safety. It's one of those deals where everybody is either blitzing or they are covering eligible receivers. Either they make a big play, or you make a big play. So Coach Bowden keeps after us on that thing, and we put it in there.

"They ran the ball, blocked it perfectly, and a guy goes about 50 or 60 yards for a score. Coach Bowden comes down there and asks what the heck is going on.

"I said, 'Coach, that's the sell-the-farm defense you wanted.'"

Bowden will take the 20 steps or so to where Andrews is running the defense from the sidelines if he spots a problem. "If we call a punt block and we go in and rough the kicker," Andrews says, "he's like, 'You aren't going to run that punt block any more. You're going to run it back.'"

Former Florida State linebackers coach Chuck Amato remembers one funny moment when Bowden questioned his use of personnel.

"We were playing BYU in the Pigskin Classic. Dulack Guerrier was third string at the time, but because of injuries he was out there playing," Amato said. "Coach Bowden came up to me and said, 'Coach, isn't that 99 a third-stringer? And I'd say, 'Yeah.'

"And he replied, 'Then what's he doing in the dadgum game?'

"And at about that time, Dulack sacks the quarterback."

Bowden says interaction with players during a game is also limited.

I don't talk to the players during a game on the sidelines very much. If one makes a great play, I might go pat him on the back. I may go up to one who is not running very hard, and say, "Son, you better start running, or you better start catching that dang ball, or you aren't playing any more."

CEO Bobby Bowden

The most important thing I learned from Bill Peterson was to hire good assistants—surround yourself with good people. Look what became of his assistants he had on his staff. Don James. Bill Parcells. John Coatta. Joe Gibbs. Vince Gibson. They went on to be pretty good head coaches.

A lot of my assistants chose to stay here for a long time. But they could have been head coaches. And some of them were head coaches. We got three former head coaches on our staff right now— Mickey [Andrews], Kevin [Steele], and Daryl Dickey have all been college head coaches.

Hiring good people plays a key role. I'm always trying to get balance. I've always been taught if everybody is the same, it's not good. If everybody is nice, it's not good. If everybody is mean, it's not good. You need a mean guy, and you need a nice guy. You need a great recruiter, and another one who is a better coach than he is recruiter. Different ages and backgrounds.

That has been so important to our success—the continuity of our staff. We've been fortunate to keep a lot of them for 10 or more years.

People wonder, "Where is Bobby?"

Well, I have a staff that has been here a long time. Plus, I got guys who have been in this position and can make decisions. Being a head coach isn't like when I first got in. You got to spend so much of your time away from game preparation—more than you would like.

I look for a coach who has a lot of ambition. A lot of coaches might be scared to hire a coach who has a lot of ambition— afraid he might get your job or something. I don't have that paranoia. I want to hire somebody who wants to get to the top, because I feel like he'll work his tail to get there.

And loyalty is so important for me. The reason why Jeffrey makes such an ideal offensive coordinator is, number one, he has what I'm looking for. There's not many coaches' sons who are not pretty good coaches. One of the toughest lessons in being a head coach is criticism. A coach's son knows that criticism is there because he's seen his daddy hung in effigy and sat in a classroom with everybody mad at his daddy. He knows the bad side, and it won't scare him.

And two, if you can't depend on your son, who can you depend on? Loyalty is such a big thing. That's the first thing we discussed when we came in here in 1976. I talked about loyalty. I talked to the staff about loyalty to me, to the university, to the president, and to the athletic director.

And another thing, there is definitely a wall there—he and I together as father and son, and he and I together as head coach and offensive coordinator. It's two different kinds of conversations. It's easier [being direct] with him than somebody else. He's mine.

The thing I did [was be tougher on my kids], and if I had my life to do over again, I might do it a little bit different. I coached every one of my sons. Steve played football for two years at West Virginia. Terry and Tommy played five years there, and Jeffrey had played five years here. The thing I did with them, I made it tougher on them than anybody else. I didn't want anybody to say he did that because he was his son. There will always be some who will say that, but I really made it tough on them.

When Tommy was a senior in high school, there was Tommy and another good receiver on that team. I gave that other one a scholarship and not Tommy. I know that hurt Tommy bad. After a year at West Virginia, this other guy quits. Tommy walks on and stays out there three years and finally we give him a scholarship and he starts his last two years. I was the same way with Terry and Jeff.

With Jeff as a coach, I try to pay no attention to that, but you are self-conscious of that.

The biggest change in my coaching since coming back to Florida State [as a head coach] is I've delegated more responsibility to the coaches. When I first started coaching, like most coaches, I was more involved. The thing about me delegating responsibility, most coaches do that. I think most coaches turn the offense over to the offense, the defense over to the defense. The head coach offers suggestions. A lot of coaches are that way. I've delegated more

The Bowden family coaching legacy continued into the next generation with Terry (left), Jeff, and Tommy (far right). (Photo courtesy of Bobby Bowden)

responsibility. I would say it became even more so when Mark Richt became offensive coordinator. Another reason is that football has become so sophisticated that as head coach you can hardly keep up with everything.

Billy [Sexton] and Mickey [Andrews] handle the [off-the-field] things. What I have always done and still do pretty much, if it's a minor problem—"You all handle it," I tell the coaches, "Y'all handle the minor stuff. If a kid is two minutes late to his meetings, don't bring that to me.

"If you can't handle it, bring it to me." If it's major, then I have to handle it. If it's any kind of major policy, I definitely run it by [athletic director] David [Hart] and T.K.

Florida State president T.K. Wetherell believes the influence of the late Bill Peterson during Bowden's three years as an

Former Florida State coaches Ed Williamson (left), Don Veller, and Bill Peterson (far right) hang out with Bowden. When Bowden was an assistant coach, he learned a lot from watching Peterson run the team. (Photo courtesy of Bobby Bowden)

assistant can't be overstated. Peterson, Florida State's head coach from 1960 to 1970, created great offenses and directed the Seminoles to their first victory over Florida. He is remembered for his malapropisms—"You guys pair off in groups of threes, then line up in a circle"—but his assistants respected him as an insightful head coach.

"One of the basic lessons in good management—what Bill Peterson taught Bowden and what Peterson taught me—is you find people who are better than you, and you make yourself the weakest link in the chain," Wetherell says. "If you do that, you've got a pretty good team. That's what Peterson did, that's what Bowden does, and that's what most good CEOs do. And that's what football coaches are these days. Find good people, let them do a job and get out of the way."

Associate head coach Mickey Andrews and assistant head coach Billy Sexton handle many of the smaller problems that come up daily in running a football program. Chuck Amato held that role before them until he left the program after the 1999 season to become head coach at North Carolina State.

"You don't need to be messing with it," Amato said. "[I used to tell Bowden,] 'If there is a problem, we'll bring it to you, and I'll keep you in tune on anything just in case anything we don't think is a problem blows up so you won't get blindsided.'"

There was another reason Bowden says he valued Amato, even though that quality could be the source of ruffled feathers between Amato and other assistants.

I'd a lot rather be challenged, and that's the one thing that Chuck Amato did so great. He was the best devil's advocate I've ever been around. Any time you wanted to do something he would say, "What if this happens and what about this?" He'd really make you think about it.

Future head coaches Amato, Brad Scott, and Tommy Bowden point to important management lessons they learned from Bobby Bowden.

"I've probably become closer to him since I left than when I was there," Amato said. "You don't realize how good he is until you are gone. Whenever there was something big, the answer just flows out of his mouth on what to do. I try to talk to him once a week during the season.

"The education he gave me was invaluable. He gives people responsibility and lets them coach and do their thing.

"He understands kids make mistakes. We all make mistakes. He would shoulder the blame instead of putting it on somebody else because he is the CEO of the program. I think most kids appreciate that. He handles things behind doors.

"He's the boss. He's more hands-on than what people think he is. He's on top of the game a lot more than what people really believe he is. He sat in [on] offensive meetings, but he would also come into the defensive room. Offensively, he was a great film watcher. I always thought he did a great job of analyzing the opposing team's defense and personnel. And he really, really studied the kicking game."

Scott observed Bowden for not only how he handled the offense, but also how he handled people.

"You had a lot of respect for him the way he dealt with you," Scott says. "He knew how people tick. He might have been tougher when we won an easy game than when we lost a heartbreaking game he knew we put everything into it."

Tommy Bowden has observed his father as a player at West Virginia and later as an assistant at Florida State.

"The biggest thing he taught me is patience and perseverance," Tommy Bowden adds. "Going through that past season [2003 at Clemson] that I did—about to get fired. He told me to be patient, work hard, and have a good staff.

"He's obviously a good coach. He can manage people. He can motivate. He's a good evaluator of talent. He's a good Xs and Os guy. All the pieces fell together. It's combination of all of that.

"I've seen the relationship he's had with his coaches. Even though it is a strong and a great coaching environment, there is still some separation between church and state."

Former assistant coach Jim Gladden says that, although Bowden gets out of his staff's way, he also makes it clear who has the final word.

"One of his greatest skills was his management skills with the staff and players and people he had to deal with," Gladden says. "In the staff meeting, he would say, 'Now there is nine of you. Each of you has a vote. If there is something we're doing you don't believe is right, I want you to speak up and let's have some devil's advocates. You have nine votes; use them. But just remember, I've got 10.'"

I get last call. I can always beat you 10-9. It's been very seldom that I had to do that with my staff.

Narrowing the Distance

When I was an assistant coach, any time I was around the head coach, there was a little tension there. Afraid you were going to do something wrong or say something wrong. So I like for my coaches to be together without me there. I nearly think they have more fun when I'm not there.

I want my coaches to have fun, and I don't know if the chemistry on this staff ain't the best we've ever had. I can tell when I travel with them and there are three or four of them in the car, they are just laughing, joking, and kidding themselves.

I always told my coaches that as much as we work together—we spend all day together, we're together at night—everybody don't like everybody, but you better act like it. Act like you like everybody. If you don't, the kids will pick up on it. They'll spot it, and then they won't be liking everybody.

We try to have that understanding. I've told them, if I ever see two of you who don't get along, I'll bring you into the office and let you all work out any problem you got. And if y'all can't work it out, I'll have to get rid of one of you. If you get the right kind of people, you don't have that kind of problem.

I called everybody in one time and said, "There he is right there, you tell [this coach] what you don't like about him. Don't tell me. Tell him." We had a good soul searching. Some of the guys came out of there in tears, but we were solid after that.

Bowden may purposely keep a measured distance from his assistants, but Mark Richt learned following the 1986 on-campus fatal shooting of offensive tackle Pablo Lopez that the door is always open.

"Pablo died, and the next day there was a team meeting he had with the players," Richt says. "I was in there and ended up being in the back of the room. He began talking about Pablo and how he wasn't sure where Pablo was going to spend eternity, and you could tell he was very distraught by it.

"He began it, 'Men, I don't preach to you guys very often, but I'm going to preach to you today.' He talked about eternal life and his life and explained his decision to become a Christian and what it meant in regard to eternity.

"[He said,] 'All you guys are 18 to 22 and think you are going to live forever, and Pablo thought the same thing. But Pablo's gone. If that was to happen to you last night, do you know where you would spend eternity?'

"I really got the sense he wished he would have had that talk before Pablo got killed. It was almost like he was saying, 'I failed to witness to him, and I'm not going to fail to witness to the rest of you.'

"He, of course, was talking to the team as a group. That's where it got me, 'The more I think about it I'm afraid where I might be going if it did happen to me last night.'

"He said, 'If any of you want to talk to me about this, my door is always open.' I went to his office and said, 'I know I'm not a player, but do you mind if I come in and talk to you about it?' I prayed to receive Christ there with him in his office."

Bowden still remembers what he told the team that day.

I pointed to an empty chair and asked, "Where is he today? Where are you going to be?" I used that as an opportunity to witness to them. What I try to do is plant a seed. I still do that.

I tell them, "Now look boys, I'm going to talk to you about something that doesn't have anything to do with football, and I want you to listen. You don't have to do what I say to do. And it doesn't have anything to do with your playing." I have had Jewish boys, and some Muslims, and I tell them they don't have to be in here when I talk about this. I excuse them.

But I feel I have a responsibility.

These other professors can get you in their classroom, and they can talk about communism—that they are communists or atheists—and nobody bothers them. I feel like as a football coach I have a right to tell you what I think is right. It's y'all's choice now. Occasionally, a kid will come in here [to the office] and talk.

[I told them,] "I want you all to go to heaven; that's why I express this. It's your choice. I don't want to die without at least telling you what I know."

Bowden cannot and does not want to separate himself from his religious associations. But he admits to not being comfortable with yet another moniker applied to him during the infancy of his coaching days at Florida State. If he had his choice of "St. Bobby," "King of the Road," and "The Riverboat Gambler," Bowden says he would have chosen "King of the Road."

It sounds more like a winner. When they named that book St. Bobby and the Barbarians [a behind-the-scenes look at the 1991 Seminoles], Ben [Brown] told me he wanted to name it that. And I said, "No. I don't think it's wise to call me that."

He said, "Well, this is what we want to do." So I called my preacher, and asked him if that is sacrilegious to call me "St. Bobby." He said, "No, all early Christians were called saints. If you were a Christian, you were called a saint." So I let [Brown] do it, but I had to check it out with my preacher first.

Part II
The Somber Side

Dealing with Death

Gunshots shattered the quiet of Florida State football in September 1986. Pablo Lopez, one of the team's most popular players, was shot and killed outside Montgomery Gym, where a fraternity dance was held on a Friday night off.

Two other active players have died during the Bowden era. Freshman Michael Hendricks died in an electrical accident near his Houston home in 1992, and another Texan, Devaughn Darling, died during an early morning workout in 2001. They represent the somber side.

I was at home, and [team chaplain] Ken Smith called me—"I'm at the hospital, and we got Pablo Lopez out here. He's been shot, and I don't think he is going to make it, so you better get out here."

I get there and go through the emergency door, and there must have been half of our players there. He had gotten shot. But our kids are not expecting him to die.

He dies, and then we got to go tell the kids. That was tragic.

Lopez's teammates had been led to the hospital's chapel, a room Bowden remembers as being not much bigger than his office. In front of him were his players, many with girlfriends.

I said, "Pablo died."

They were just screaming, and laying on the floor, and kicking the floor. I didn't know people responded like this over a death. That must have gone on for 10 minutes.

It was my first experience around a minority race when somebody dies. This group's custom is to do this, and this group's custom is to do that. I didn't know this would be the reaction the kids would have. Since that time I've been to a funeral at a black church, and people cried out. They are more animated while we're more silent. It's their way of doing it.

The other thing I'll always remember, when we went to the funeral in Miami, a good proportion of the Miami football team was there. Pablo knew all those kids from high school. That was very impressive to me that their football players came. I bet nearly all their first team was there. I think that is one reason we've always had a good relationship with Miami.

Lopez had married just before his death, and his wife later gave birth to their child. Bowden admits he lost track of the family.

I sure would like to see his son one day. One of these days I'll sure try to do that.

Freshman linebacker Devaughn Darling died the morning of February 26, 2001, after he collapsed at the end of an off-season conditioning drill. A conclusive cause of death was not reached by the medical examiner's office. His twin brother, Devard, a wide receiver for Florida State, was later told he would not be cleared by Florida State team physicians to continue his career with the Seminoles, and he transferred to Washington State. He played without incident and was selected in the 2004 NFL draft.

That's the worst thing to happen. To lose a player [Devaughn] like that. We'd never had anything like that.

And having to tell Devard Darling he could not play was bad. That hurt bad. I did that right here in the office. "The doctors won't let you play. We're doing what is best for you. We're just afraid something might happen to you." He was very quiet and wasn't the kind of person who would fuss at somebody. But I'm sure when he left he was disappointed.

That's always tough when a kid wants to play more than anything. That's always tough for me, and that goes back to my childhood. Because I had rheumatic fever, and the doctor told me not to play. I always remember that he said, "If you play, you'll be dead by the time you're 40." So when I couldn't play, my family decided to go find another doctor. And we found a heart specialist in Birmingham, and he said I could play.

So that is one reason it was so hard with Devard. The other thing, I had talked to him before I got the verdict that we can't let him play. I had talked to him about, "Look, you got your career ahead of you. You got to do it [play] for your brother." And then

Bowden speaks at Devaughn Darling's memorial service. (Photo by Phil Coale/Sunset Images)

when I finally had to call him and tell him he couldn't play, it really hurt. Because I felt like he was like me when I was 13 when the doctor said I couldn't play.

In a memorial held in Florida State's Ruby Diamond Auditorium, Bowden paid tribute to Devaughn Darling's work ethic. "I hope this won't hit anyone the wrong way … but he's the first player I've coached in 47 years who actually worked himself to death," Bowden told the 1,000 people in attendance. "He said, 'I will not quit. I will die before I give up.'"

It would be one of two times in as many years when Bowden's intent would be questioned for what he believed was a sincere tribute. Bowden was also questioned when he came up with the idea of using "Let's Roll" as the 2002 team's slogan. The words were spoken by Todd Beamer, a passenger on United Flight 93 that crashed into the Pennsylvania countryside on September 11, 2001. Beamer said the words before he and other passengers apparently took action to thwart terrorists from crashing the plane into the White House. Florida State put the words on its practice shirts that were not sold to the public. It earned Bowden criticism from the media and fans. But the chief executive director of the Todd Beamer Foundation later embraced the tribute.

I couldn't understand [the reaction to my comments about Darling]. Really, what I was doing was bragging on him. That he worked so hard, a lesser guy would have quit. He was such a hard worker it probably would have been better if he wasn't a hard worker.

I compare that to "Let's Roll." That surprised me that it became an issue all over the nation. I'd think a lot stronger before I'd do something like that again. But I thought that was perfect in honor of the guys that died. I was very surprised of all the negative stuff.

A Death Threat

Days before Florida State was to play South Carolina in 1990 in Columbia, South Carolina, Bowden's longtime administrative assistant, Sue Hall, received a letter. The individual threatened Bowden's life, and Bowden learned later it was believed to be a person who had lost money wagering on the Seminoles. Hall didn't tell her boss but handed the letter over to Billy Smith, who oversaw Bowden's security at home and on the road. Florida State won the November game 41-10.

Bowden's recollection was that he didn't know about the threat until after the game.

Bill stayed mighty close to me. I couldn't hardly walk out the door without him being right there by me.

Smith said he informed Bowden about it the Wednesday or Thursday before the game at South Carolina. But Smith never got the idea it fazed Bowden before or during the game.

"From all indications from [the person's] letter he had apparently lost quite a bit of money from the game we played before," Smith says. "He wrote that at the next out-of-town game, 'I'm going to get you.' It had a Pittsburgh, Pennsylvania, address. I went to Coach and told him, I said, 'I want to tell you up front that the President of the United States has got the best security in the world, and they get shot at every once in a while. I'm going to do everything I can to make sure that doesn't happen to you. However, the main thing I need you to do is you coach the football game, and you let me handle the other part of it and maybe when it's over with, we'll both be happy.'

"I don't think it really soaked in with Coach Bowden. I don't really think it meant anything to him until after the ballgame was over. I backed the trooper's car up as close to the [locker] room as we could possibly get it. I told him, 'As soon as you get showered and dressed, we are not going to sign autographs. You and I and couple of troopers are going to get out of here and go to the airport.' We walk out the door and there are 132 law enforcement officers standing in single or double file to escort him out to the car.

"He told me, 'When I walked out that door and saw all those law enforcement guys, my heart sunk.'"

More recently, Bowden received another death threat from a man who also made one to the president. That threat was handled without the knowledge of the media.

At West Virginia, Bowden was hung in effigy in 1974. And a death threat was called into his Morgantown, West Virginia, home that was overheard by his teenage daughter, Ginger. And another individual took a swing at Bowden as he walked of the Mountaineers' home field.

The death threat made against Bowden before the South Carolina game apparently did not come from a Florida State fan, and Bowden says he hasn't had bad experiences with Seminoles fans since arriving in Tallahassee.

I guess I haven't made people so mad here. The only thing we had like that here was when [South Carolina coach] Jim Carlen was coming over to me after the game in 1979 to shake hands. Somebody who had played for him and thought Jim had done him wrong hit him with a fist. Pow.

Interestingly, the person who hit Carlen was actually a Florida State baseball player who was upset with how Carlen had dealt with his brother, a football player under Carlen. Florida State baseball coach Mike Martin says handling that incident became his first official duty as the newly named baseball coach for the Seminoles that fall.

Bowden says he never worried about his safety or confrontations with fans, even on the road. But there was at least one memorable moment in Gainesville—in 1991.

A lot of times I'll go play somebody and find a penny. I've had that happen a lot of times. So we're down at Gainesville, and there on the sidelines is a penny and I pick it up. Well, there's another penny, and I see another one and realized they are throwing pennies at us. Our kids complained about getting hit by the pennies.

It was at Florida Field where Bowden appeared close to resigning following a 53-14 loss in 1983 to the Gators—the fifth defeat in a row in Gainesville. Assistant coach Brad Scott says he doesn't recall Bowden being more upset than after that game.

In his disappointment after the game, Bowden said, "If I can't find a way to beat them, I think enough of Florida State to say maybe they ought to find someone better."

When pressed on his comments, he added, "Right now, I just can't think of anybody."

That line—"I couldn't think of somebody better"—I got that from Bear [Bryant]. He said that one time.

If I ever talked about [retiring or resigning], it was just a moment of despair. Not putting any thought to it. We got totally embarrassed [in that game].

In *The Bowden Way*, the bestselling book he coauthored with his son Steven, Bowden allowed that he had considered stepping down if his son Jeff was not hired as offensive coordinator in 2001.

"The issue was more serious than I allowed to be known," Bobby Bowden wrote in the book. "I was frustrated enough over this nepotism issue to consider retiring if my decision was overruled."

But even then, Bowden says, he didn't seriously consider retiring. Nor did he when his program came under criticism from the media in 2003 in the wake of the arrests of Adrian McPherson and Darnell Dockett and a gambling investigation by local law enforcement.

I wouldn't dare retire over something like that [media criticism]. I can be as tough as anybody else wants to be. This comes with the territory. I got to keep reminding myself of that.

[As for son Jeff's hiring], even if I said it then, I don't think I even thought about retiring. [Former Florida State president] Bernie Sliger had told me it was OK to hire Jeffrey. On the nepotism thing, you get special permission from your president and Bernie had given me special permission to hire him, so I didn't see any problem making him coordinator. The new president [Sandy D'Alemberte] said, "No, you can't do that." I could see where he was coming from.

How all this happened is this—when Mark [Richt] left, I wanted to stay within the staff if I could. We're going to run my offense. I had been here [26] years

[Offensive coordinators] George Haffner, George Henshaw, Wayne McDuffie, Brad Scott, Mark Richt, and Jeff Bowden. They're going to run my offense. So I don't need somebody to come in here and tell me how to run new stuff.

When Mark left, my thinking was Billy Sexton or Jeff. Bill had been here longer, but I felt like Bill would be better in the administrative stuff. So I told Bill I'm going to work you in as an assistant head coach and give Jeffrey the offensive coordinator job. I thought that was all there was to it because Dr. Sliger had already approved of me hiring Jeff [as receivers coach]. So when I hired Jeff [the first time], he approved it right off the bat. When the offensive coordinator job came open, it's my prerogative and I'll make him offensive coordinator. I told Dave Hart about it, and he said, "We better kind of go slow on that."

And I thought, "Why go slow? This is what I want to do." Dave Hart informed D'Alemberte about it, and it was against his principles. One thing about him is that he had principles. So we go up to his office, and D'Alemberte said, "When Jeff was assistant coach, he wasn't working directly under you. Now as offensive coordinator he is working under you, and we can't have that." He wouldn't bend. So we worked it out where we made Mickey Andrews the associate head coach, and he has to answer to Mickey. I appreciated him doing that because he could have just said, "No."

Part III
Pen Pals, the Press, and the Public

Mr. Postman

I try to answer all my mail. Now if it's nasty, it won't even get to me. I have orders to not even let me see that kind of mail.

A lot may be seeking an autograph. One I will always remember is there was a kid who entered a pig in the Future Farmers of America contest or fair. He was writing me to brag that he had won. I have never met him. He sent a picture of the pig. He had named it after me—Bobby.

I've had hogs, horses, and dogs named for me. And I've had streets. When I first came to Florida State—I hadn't been here a year yet—and a guy from this town near Lake Okeechobee named a street after me. And I hadn't done anything here yet.

I have regular writing sessions with prisoners. They write me a letter, and I'll write them back. I might send them a program. I might send them a Bible or religious book. For years and years and years I've done that. Just two days ago [in late May 2004] I got a letter from a guy who has been in prison for I don't know how long. I have probably been corresponding with him for 10 years. He'll write me a letter, and I'll answer it.

Somebody is always sending me some kind of religious book, and when I get through with it, I send it off to someone and then they'll use it in prison.

That's just something we've done and hadn't really said anything about.

I'm afraid it will get out.

Bowden laughs.

He knows the idea of him being a pen pal to prisoners will become fodder for jokes because of past Florida State players who have run afoul of the law. Bowden built a reputation as a media favorite for years because of legendary access. He was one of the first to grant sideline interviews during the game and one of the last to close the locker room to the media after games. And at the end of the 2003 season, Florida State remains one of a handful of football programs that allowed full access the morning after games and nearly every day leading up to the game. Bowden meets the beat writers who regularly report on the football program every day but Friday.

But in 2003, Bowden took measures that many in the media viewed as punitive. For a period of time he made himself less available to the media in general and unavailable to some reporters.

I might get mad [at a reporter] for writing something, and then it goes away. It don't last long. I don't ever believe in vengeance. I don't think I carry grudges.

Yet Bowden admits that there have been times at Florida State when he has not granted requests made by certain media members but that practice became national news in 2003 and he has continued that policy in 2004 with some individuals.

Some people, I say, I don't like, but I don't hate anybody. There might be two or three. There are some writers I don't want anything to do with—they call me [for an interview], and they can't have it. I've had TV people call me, and I won't give them an interview. But I don't hate them. I just don't like the way they treated me.

His interaction during the season with the public beyond signing autographs and shaking hands has always been limited to a Monday luncheon and a weekly call-in show. And that goes for high-placed boosters, too. Bowden says he's never had an inner circle of alumni and fans that he socializes with at Florida State. Tommy Bowden said it's something other coaches could learn from his father.

"Once you develop a close relationship, they want to think they can call some shots and have your ear," Tommy says. "You don't have time to schmooze guys. He was probably a little bit ahead of his time. Probably a lot of coaches realize now they had better withdraw a little bit from extracurricular activity with money guys."

Part IV
Relationships with Players

A Lesson Learned

In my last game at Howard College, we were getting ready to go out and play, and our coach told us that he kicked seven guys off the team. The state fair was in Birmingham, and he told us, "Don't go."

Seven guys did, and he found out about it. He kicked the guys off the team, and we lost a game where I thought we could have won.

It made an impression on me. I know it sounds like a fairy tale, but, really, it did. I'm always teaching team first. When our coach kicked all of them boys off the team, he punished the whole team.

I always said that, if I have something like that, I'll find another way to punish the player. There's been so many times I've disciplined where nobody knows about that. I've kicked kids out of the dorm. "You can't act right—you pay for your own. We will take you off the training table—go pay for your own meals."

I'm going to discipline them, but I'm not going to kick them off the team if I can help it.

There are times where I've had to kick them off and say, "I just can't keep you any more." If I ever tell a kid "I'm going to give you one more chance, and that's all," then that's what I'm going to do.

A lot of times if we have to make a decision about a player or something, I'll go in with the staff and say, "This is what is happening. I would like to hear what you say before I make a decision."

People want to know, what can we do to stop football players from doing wrong? It's people. When will it change? When society changes. Our morals have dropped so low. A kid does wrong, but he doesn't think it's wrong. He ain't been taught it's wrong. He may have been taught they owe this to me. They overcharged. I think it reflects the way our society has changed over the last 28 years since I've been here.

Bowden's practice of giving second chances to his players who run afoul of the law or team rules has its critics. Decisions regarding Adrian McPherson, Sebastian Janikowski, Laveranues Coles, and Peter Warrick—among others—received nationwide scrutiny by the media. But Bowden insists he would handle the situations the same way the second time around.

Bowden started McPherson at quarterback against North Carolina State in 2002 after McPherson had informed Florida State assistant coaches prior to the game that he was in some trouble. McPherson was dismissed from the team two days later amid a police investigation into alleged involvement in check forgery. He later pleaded no contest in the case and received probation.

If you didn't play him and you found out that he was correct in what he told us but you already ruled him guilty, that wouldn't have been right.

If I had known the truth, I couldn't have played him. As soon as I knew what happened, I went to Dave Hart. I tell my players—

"I ain't going to lie to y'all, and I don't want you lying to me. We can't afford to be lying to each other. Now if you ever lie to me, it means I can't trust you any more."

Bowden was accused of practicing double standards when he allowed Florida State's best athlete, Peter Warrick, to remain on the team in 1999 while dismissing another receiver, Laveranues Coles, after they allegedly received an illegal discount on merchandise. Warrick missed two games and returned to the team after pleading to misdemeanor theft after a security camera caught Coles and Warrick on camera getting $421.38 in designer clothes for $21.70.

It's made like I kicked [Coles] off and kept the best one. He was as good as anybody, but he had strikes against him. I told him, if you cut any more classes... He had been slighting academics, and he had some trouble that didn't involve football but family. The thing that really got me had to do with academics.

Perhaps no disciplinary action received more national attention than Bowden's response to kicker Sebastian Janikowski's breaking curfew prior the 2000 Sugar Bowl, which Florida State won over Virginia Tech to earn the national title.

That wasn't the first bowl game he broke curfew at. Just nobody knew about it before—we took care of the discipline, and nothing was said of it.

When we went to the Sugar Bowl, we knew that the night his gal was coming to town he was going to miss curfew. We knew. Sure enough he missed it, and we got him. When a guy breaks curfew, we put him on 9 o'clock curfew for the rest of the time and then we run it out of him.

Some thought we did nothing and let him by. But that's just the way we handled that kind of thing, and I would guess that's how a lot of people do that.

I messed that one up. I volunteered that [information]. All the writers were around me, and they wanted something. And I couldn't think of nothing to tell them. Well, we had three kids miss curfew, one maybe two minutes late, another five minutes late, and the other guy was long-time late. That was Sebastian. I talked to Mickey [Andrews]. We ran them all, and Mickey said he wasn't going to start so-and-so. Well, we didn't do that with Janikowski.

So I was asked, "Are you going to bench him?"

"No, I'm going to start him." That's when I came up with the international rule and everybody got on me about that. If I hadn't volunteered information, nobody would have known. I don't think we were wrong in the way we handled curfews.

Of course, not everyone agreed. Bowden was criticized throughout the media for starting Janikowski under what he had jokingly called the "Warsaw Rule."

"Coach has taken an awful lot of abuse—that he's a phony, [that] ... he can't be as good as he says he is, and that the religious stuff is a bunch of bull," former assistant coach Jim Gladden says. "It's not. He is a simple man who believes he has been blessed.

"I always felt like Coach had an unbelievable amount of good judgment and wisdom. Not every decision in the long run turned out right, because they all don't."

"I always liked the fact he treats his players like his children," adds Peter Boulware, a consensus All-American in 1996 selected in the first round of the 1997 NFL Draft. "Every player he had—'This is my kid, and I'm going to bat for him.' Any time a player got into a tough situation or it was hard for a player, he went to bat for a player. He treated us like his own.

"That's why I love him and why the players love him. He's willing to take the criticism from other people and say, 'You know what, these are my players; these are my kids, and I don't care what anybody says. You can ridicule me, you can talk about my reputation, but I'm going to bat for them.' And that's why I really have respect for him."

An Open Door

Bobby Bowden had a present for his fifth-year seniors prior to the opening of the 1987 spring practice. They wouldn't have to practice. But, as tight end Pat Carter quickly realized, that didn't apply to seniors such as Carter who had played three consecutive seasons since arriving at Florida State.

"I was going into my senior year, but I had to practice. I was really upset because I had played as a freshman and played more than all those other [fifth-year] guys. Coach Bowden always told us we could come see him anytime—that his door was open.

"Well, he must have known I was coming. I go into his office and say, 'Coach Bowden, I need to talk to you.' I sit down and say, 'Look, I don't think it's fair that you are making me practice and I played more than all of these guys.'

"I can't remember what he said. I just remember leaving his office really ready to play spring football. He could [affect] you like that."

Carter's impulse to rush up to Bowden's office to speak his mind was exactly what the head coach wants from his players.

You don't want them fearing you. I want their respect. I always want it where they can come in here and talk with me. But that's not natural for a kid to do. I wasn't that way. I couldn't go talk to my coach. I was either too shy, or I didn't feel like I should.

Yet I want my kids to always know they can come and talk with me. Some kids will come in here to Florida State and talk to me like I told them they could. But after a year or two, they won't do it any more. I guess they feel like other kids would think they would come in to get favors. That they were apple-polishing the coach.

Now [former fullback] William Floyd would come through a lot. And so would Warrick Dunn and Todd Williams.

Todd Williams briefly lived on the streets in Dade County as a teenager after the grandmother who raised him in Bradenton, Florida, died. He admitted to stealing and breaking into places to sleep. After he returned to Bradenton, he supported himself with odd jobs and the help of a local church. He was a gamble for Bowden and his staff when they signed him to play on the offensive line in 1998. He had anger management issues and no male role model in his life.

When he graduated in 2002 and then went on to the NFL, Williams credited Bowden.

Todd would come in [my office] all the time, especially when he first came here, because he didn't have anybody. I would always feel a little softer for those kind of guys. I tried to talk to them about staying out of trouble. I would give him talks about what you can't do. "You can't do that. Control yourself."

When we recruited him, the people who talked most favorably about him were his teachers. When we had to visit him, we had to do it at school. He didn't have anybody. We visited him in the library with the coach and several of his teachers. They just felt he would not fail, although they knew he had done some things that were scary. He was a "yes sir, no sir" kind of guy. He came up here and graduated.

The best advice I can give to a player is to put your education first. And most do. But there are always some who only want to play football. I always try to tell them to get their priorities right. And do their best.

I try to tell them, "You don't want to look back and say, 'If I only had done this.'" There are underachievers and overachievers. Underachiever is the worst description people can give you. I think that goes back to me being the runt of the litter.

I tell this to my kids—every kid goes through a day of reckoning—a day where he has to decide to play football or no, I'm not going to play any more. And like with anything, if you are going to do it, do it with your best. Make it your worthwhile. This can be a very tough, very demanding sport.

Bowden, seen here in uniform at Woodlawn High School, established himself as an overachiever. That's a goal he sets for every Florida State player. (Photo courtesy of Bobby Bowden)

It happened with me as a sophomore in high school, and I weighed 116 pounds. My first year out there, I was on the B team scrimmaging the varsity. I was playing defensive back, and they ran a play and somebody just comes up and blindsides me and just knocks me from there to here. And I'm thinking, "This is football?" I had to decide right there whether I wanted to play or not. But I decided to play

But on overachievers and underachievers, maybe the greatest asset Bear Bryant had was to make kids overachieve. The old expression, he could take "his'n and beat your'n and take your'n and beat his'n." I could do that probably to an extent.

Warrick Dunn, whose mother, a police officer, was killed before his freshman year while working off-duty, often talked to Bowden about being a father to his five siblings. They were being raised by their grandmother in Baton Rouge, Louisiana, and had no father figure at home. Dunn was trying to play that role from long distance.

I remember when he came into my office the first time—you just wanted to grab and hug him like a child. He and I hit it off right off the bat.

He nearly had to be the father to the brothers and sisters. I remember one day he came in my office, sat right there in that chair, and said, "I really got a problem."

I asked him, "What's the matter?"

He said, "My younger brother is not doing right. School and stuff. I don't know what to do."

I told him, "You just ought to go home and get him straight. You're the daddy now, and you got to treat him like a child."

And he went home for a couple of days.

Dunn's jersey was retired for his exploits at Florida State, which included nearly 4,000 rushing yards. He played for the Tampa Bay Buccaneers and now plays for the Atlanta Falcons.

He received national recognition for his "Homes for the Holidays" project in which he pays the down payment on homes for single mothers. He also completely furnishes the houses.

"There were times I had to go home for disciplinary reasons because my brothers and sisters weren't doing well in school or they were just acting like kids," Dunn said. "They had to be disciplined. He was good about letting me go home to handle those situations. I would ask him for advice on 'how you would handle this situation.' And he would give me different instances and his opinion—to use it the best way I could. And I did. It meant a lot to me that he understood.

"He respected what I was trying to do because I wasn't a guy that was getting in trouble. I was going to class and doing the little things. And at the same time he knew I had a big responsibility at home. When I signed to come to Florida State, I think he knew right then he had to take on that responsibility [to offer advice on handling family matters].

"He meant a lot to me. Most coaches, it isn't easy to talk to them. But he was an easy person, and he has your back no matter what happens. This is a guy that I respect and admire and didn't know much about before I went to Florida State. When I got there, I started to understand why players love to play for him. I cherish the relationship we do have—it's special and unique."

Not every player who comes to Bowden's office does so by choice. Wrongdoing will result in a visit. So will suspicion on Bowden's part that things aren't right with a particular player. In the spring of 2003, Bowden gave notice to Darnell Dockett that his Florida State career was in jeopardy following his arrest for allegedly accepting illegally discounted merchandise. But Bowden says that years earlier he had suggested to Dockett that he might think about playing elsewhere.

I brought him in here one time and told him he might take off if he wanted to. We were going to move him from defensive end to tackle because we thought he would be a better tackle. So we told

*him, "Son, you are going to have to move to tackle." I told him
Odell [Haggins, a current Florida State assistant coach] had done
that years ago and become an All-American.*

*He wasn't with us [on that]. So I told him, "You might as
well take off"—go somewhere else. He called his uncle [who raised
him], and I talked to his uncle and told him, "Look, the guy will
be better at tackle. You got to trust us."*

*And the uncle agreed, and so [Darnell] came back and said,
"Coach, I'm staying."*

*I try to sell him [on switching positions] first, and, at last
resort, I'll tell him you got to do it. I haven't had to do that too often.*

Quarterback Chris Rix is another player who has made his
share of visits to Bowden's office. Rix, already one of Florida
State's most prolific quarterbacks entering his senior season in
2004, found himself in the coach's office for tardiness to meetings; missing final exams, which cost him a start in the 2003
Sugar Bowl; and parking in a handicapped parking spot that
drew national attention during the 2003 season.

Rix was a hot topic on Bowden's 2004 Seminoles Boosters
tour.

*Everybody asks about Chris Rix. "Why do you start him?
Why do you play him?" It goes back to not being prejudiced. I
thought he was the best quarterback we had. With the parking stuff
and sleeping late, missing class—it was carelessness, common-sense
stuff. He and I have spent a lot of time in this office talking through
the years.*

*Just carelessness. He's got an agenda and does it. I think he's
grown up a lot. First year he won eight and then he had 10 wins
his redshirt junior year, so really he's about on schedule as a redshirt
junior. Those first couple of years were a struggle. As quarterback,
we would expect him to set the example. Any time he did any of
those things—we would punish him, make him get up, and run
stadium steps, but it wasn't big enough to kick him off the team.*

Bowden and Penn State coach Joe Paterno kick back during the 2004 off season when they hooked up at the annual Nike coaches outing. (Photo courtesy of Bobby Bowden)

Bowden allows he doesn't have as many stories about his Florida State football players as he does about recruiting, games, and his staff.

"If they come to him for advice he'll give it," his wife, Ann, says. "He's available for them, but he doesn't seek them out."

Bowden says he'll never forget Florida State's trip to the 1989 Sugar Bowl when he shared a bench with Odell Haggins at the front of a New Orleans steamboat. Florida State had just one loss that year but was not in a position to play for the national championship. Bowden was concerned that his team might not be into the game.

We're on a cruise on the Mississippi, and I'm at the front of the boat—me and Odell. I'm worrying about the game. And Odell said, "Coach, don't worry about them. We got 'em." That really built my confidence because I thought our kids were down and maybe not up for it. When Odell told me that, it really made me feel good.

Florida State won 13-7.

Wherever Bowden can be found, he says his door remains open. But there is a distance he maintains.

I would think my relationships with my players in my more than 50 years of coaching have been a relationship of big brother, daddy, and granddaddy. I'm in the granddaddy stage [now]. When I started off, I was as young as the players were. I was an assistant at Howard, and I had to coach boys that I played with. I kind of had to stand back. I couldn't run around with them. I couldn't go to dances with them. I had to be more like a big brother to them.

As I've gotten older, I've gotten a little more fatherly. I didn't do that when I was young. There's no doubt about that. Coach Bryant was that way and then at the end was soft. I think that comes with age.

You look at them as you would your own son. But, of course, they are not. If a player is having some kind of personal problem, I would tell him, "If you were my son, I wouldn't even give you a choice; I would want you to do this. But you're not my son. You got to talk to your parents and decide what's best."

I keep up with them, but I don't correspond with them much. They might contact me. Usually, I'll run into them when I travel. It's not like I write them all the time. Some will come by after they leave. The guys who went on to the NFL and come back on their weekend off. That kind of thing.

A kid writes you 10 years later—"I didn't realize at the time what you meant. I thank you for what you said. I'm married, and I got children and tell them to do the same thing you told me."

How would I like to be remembered among the players? The biggest thing is that he treated us fairly. Not equally. But fairly. Just that I treat them fairly.

Joe Paterno and I have talked about this before. You can't treat them all equally. If a guy is first-team fullback, I can't give the fourth-team fullback the same amount of practice. They can't all have equal opportunity.

Octavis Jackson and Bowden share a laugh at Media Day. (Photo by Phil Coale/Sunset Images)

Pants Down to Here

With his ever-present notepad in hand, Bobby Bowden watched the 1998 preseason practice from the familiar observation point of his tower. Something caught his eye as he surveyed his team warming up, and Octavis Jackson soon was invited to the tower to see whether he noticed the same thing. Jackson was one of just two players attending a practice with a large afro.

I asked him—"Doesn't that one player look different? I'd like everybody to look the same—neatly kept hair." He got the message.

Bowden, who as a teenager once bleached his hair on a trip to Panama City and then tried to hide the "experiment" from his mother, says the message he delivers to players today is the same he delivered to his first Florida State team in 1976 as a fiery and intense young coach. It's just that he's turned down the volume and adjusted the tone.

Although Bowden may discourage a player from wearing an afro, the latest 'dos such as corn rows and dreadlocks are allowed. Earrings are OK around the football offices, but not on the football field. Even the habit of wearing pants well below the point of good taste is tolerated.

And tolerance, say Bowden's current and former coaches, is the key to his success.

"That's the secret of Bobby Bowden—is that he is still old school, but he is smart enough to allow change," former offensive coordinator Brad Scott says. "He'll challenge you just to see how much you believe in it. But he allows change. And it's not just offense, but things like earrings. In some areas he was ahead of the game for an old school coach."

Another former coach, Jim Gladden, agrees.

"He has changed to some degree in how he deals with the players," Gladden adds. "He has become more tolerant. I don't want to say lenient or easy, but he has become more tolerant of the cultural differences.

"I think a key to Coach's resilience is that he has been flexible. The better word is that he is tolerant. Tolerance is the word with him."

Bowden uses the term "less crusty."

I was less sympathetic. I was tougher on the kids. Wouldn't put up with nothing. Each year that chipped off a little bit. You finally realize, "Don't cut off your nose to spite your face." Through the years I've gained on that. If this kid did something wrong, don't kick him off the team. Make him do this or that. Then if he can't do it, you got to let him go.

When I first started, he was gone.

Bowden, the biker. (Photo courtesy of Bobby Bowden)

Bowden, the country boy. (Photo by Phil Coale/Sunset Images)

Athletes have changed, too. I think the biggest change in athletes—I don't think they are as mentally tough. I know they are not. They are better physically—faster, bigger and stronger, and probably smarter—but they are not as mentally tough as they use to be.

It's because everybody got smarter. When I first started playing and coaching, it's nearly as if you didn't have injuries. "Son, you got a bad knee there, but it will be OK. We'll put a brace on it, and you play with it." I can remember having a high hip pointer in high school, and I could hardly walk. I never missed a day of practice. I did everything everybody else did. They put a sponge on it and a big hip pad on it. It was about to kill me. Nowadays, if a kid has a hip pointer, he's out two weeks. So they aren't as tough. But we were tough out of ignorance. We're smarter now.

I might have been the first coach—I can't prove it—who gave players water on the field. When I first came up, you could not have water. When I became head coach, I thought, "Well, when you play a game, you have water on the sideline and kids come get water. Why in practice can I not let them have water?" That was in '55 at South Georgia College.

Athletes have changed in other ways [since first arriving at Florida State]. You have to keep up with cultures. I never single out anybody, but I do talk about morals, what is morally accepted and what is not. Kids with kids. That one, naturally, has been difficult for me. I believe so strongly in family, father and wife and children. You love their children no matter what. I usually asked them, "Are you going to marry them?" But I never get on them about it again. The atmosphere of society has changed, which means the people you get have changed.

I have been through it all—first long hair and then back to short. Then earrings came in. Those were the two biggest ones. Now dreadlocks—I think they are good, because it's neat. I've gotten used to it.

Another [style] change is wearing britches down real low. Boy, that's a change.

I've thought about it that one day before I retire, I'm going to walk out on that practice field wearing an earring and wearing my britches down to here. You know, I'm just going to do that.

Now, that will be a story to tell.